PLAY UP, HIGHER WALTON!

Football in a Lancashire village from 1882 to 2005

by

Peter Holme

Landy Publi...
2006

10107884-2

ISBN 1-872895-67-0

A catalogue record of this book is available from the British Library

Layout by Peter Holme
Printed by Nayler Group, Aero Mill, Church, Accrington
Tel 01254 234247

Published by Landy Publishing, "Acorns", 3 Staining Rise, Staining, Blackpool FY3 0BU Tel/Fax 01253 895678
who have also published:-

Traipsing from a Lancashire Toll Bar; Bretherton, Croston, Hoole, Hesketh Bank, Tarleton & Walmer Bridge in Focus
                              by Betty Gilkes & Stan Pickles

Life on the Lancaster Canal   by Janet Rigby

Lancashire's Medieval Monasteries   by Brian Marshall

Preston in Focus   by Stephen Sartin

Blackburn in Focus   by Alan Duckworth & Jim Halsall

A Blackburn Childhood in Wartime by Marjorie Clayton

Blackburn's Shops at the Turn of the Century by Matthew Cole

Glimpses of Glasson Dock & Vicinity by Ruth Z. Roskell

A full list of publications will be sent on request.

INTRODUCTION

Higher Walton is a small village in Lancashire on the outskirts of Preston. Its main claim to fame is that it is the birthplace (in 1912) of the great opera singer Kathleen Ferrier. I moved to the village in 1980 and although I am a football fan, I never watched the Higher Walton team who played in the local Preston & District League. Twenty years later I was looking through a football annual from 1885 when I noticed that a Higher Walton team had entered the first round of the FA Cup in that season. This made me curious and I wanted to find out more. Further investigation showed that they had played in the Lancashire League in the 1890s and were its very first champions. They played games against much bigger clubs such as Accrington, Bury, Blackpool, Burnley and Bolton Wanderers. In 1889 they even reached the final of the Lancashire Cup, beating Football League opposition (Blackburn Rovers and Everton) along the way. I decided to do some more research, using archive material from newspapers and other sources to build up a better picture of the team and its achievements. The search for personal recollections eventually led me to meet some descendants of the early players and to speak to others who have been associated with Higher Walton teams in more recent times.

This book describes many of the games played by the first Higher Walton football team in Victorian times, and then follows the fortunes of other Higher Walton teams up to the present day. It does not aim to be a complete statistical history but tries to tell the story of all the teams and players. In the past 120 years there have been four distinct Higher Walton teams: the first Victorian team (1882-95), Higher Walton Albion (1895-1913), Higher Walton in the Preston YMCA league (1920-40) and Higher Walton United in the Preston & District League and Blackburn Combination (1953-2005).

Sadly, we can no longer speak to anyone who saw Higher Walton play in Victorian times. We have to rely on written sources of information such as football annuals or newspapers to find fixtures, results and match reports. Preston in the 1880s and 1890s had three main newspapers: the *'Preston Guardian'*, the *'Preston Herald'* and the *'Lancashire Daily Post'*. Reports of these early football matches vary in quality and during the cricket season football took a back seat, so it is not always easy to find out all the details of players and games in those far-off times.

The first part of this history tells the story of the rise and fall of the Victorian Higher Walton team. It describes how football was played in those times: the rules, tactics and equipment. It includes some of the famous teams and top players who played against Higher Walton in those early years. The story continues through the decades up to the present day as other Higher Walton teams carried the footballing torch.

Many people have helped me with this history. I am indebted to football historian Gordon Small who has also researched the Victorian Higher Walton team and provided information about the the East Lancs Charity Shield and guest players. I am grateful to the National Football Museum for allowing me to use their archives. Journalist Ian Mather located newspaper articles in the Colindale Library, London. The late Harry Mather allowed me to photograph his grandfather's medals and Norman Hayes loaned the photograph of Higher Walton Albion. Marlene Short gave me information about her grandfather, Hubert Woods, who was secretary in the 1930s, and let me copy team photographs. George Rounding provided information about the Clarke family and allowed me to photograph their medals. Gill Dimmock provided photographs and information about her grandfather, John Taberner. Rita and John Massam provided images from their large collection of photographs. The late Frank Counsell was a mine of information about the post-war period and Harold Wilson provided team photographs from the 1970s. I am very grateful to Fred Southern of the Lancashire FA who let me look at his 'Preston & District League' handbooks. Jim and Lilian Howarth provided information on the 'Blackburn & District Football Combination'. Roy Rich of the Preston & District League supplied photographs. Dick Clegg, the Preston schools football historian, provided tables from 'Lancashire Daily Post' handbooks. Malcolm Crowther supplied information about the most recent Higher Walton team. Some photographs were supplied by the late Bob Burns and  the information on Higher Walton village and school was provided by Miss Anne Bradley. Thank you to Bob Dobson for his help and encouragement, and to Dian Holme for diligently checking the manuscript. Thank you, everyone! An appendix of all results for the period 1882 to 1892 and league tables from 1891 to 2005 will be deposited at the Harris reference library and Lancashire Record Office if you are interested in the detailed statistics.

Peter Holme

SETTING THE SCENE

Higher Walton is a small village which lies three miles to the south east of Preston on the A675 to Blackburn. As you leave Preston you first cross the River Ribble at Walton-le-Dale, where Oliver Cromwell once led his army. The road continues on the flat for a mile or so, passing houses and fields, then under the M6 motorway, until it reaches an imposing Victorian cotton mill on the banks of the River Darwen. This is surrounded by rows of terraced houses, a few shops and a prominent church on the hill. The first name given to this village was *'Moon's Mill'* but after 1860 it became known as *'Higher Walton'*. It very much owes its existance to the cotton industry of the nineteenth century.

The mill on the Darwen.

The river Darwen flows swiftly from Blackburn and joins the River Ribble at Preston. This abundance of water power meant that a corn mill was built near the river, where Higher Walton stands today, and this became known as *'Moon's Mill'*. By 1799 part of this water-powered mill was being used for the manufacture of textiles. The mill needed a greater number of workers, so the village began to grow. An 1823 report into child labour mentioned *"Mr James Livesey's cotton factory at Moon's Mill in Walton-le-Dale......There are about 130 persons employed here, and several under 9 years of age..... There is a Sunday School attached to the factory at which the children are taught gratuitiously"*.

The Rodgett legacy.

In 1850 a new steam powered spinning mill was built on the same site by the Rodgett family, who lived in a large Georgian-style house called *'Darwen Bank'* which was situated off Cottage Lane, Bamber Bridge. The main house has been demolished, but the gatehouse still stands. The mill owner was Miles Rodgett, and his sons Edward and Richard ran the mill. The family owned much of the land and property in the village. They were enlightened employers and looked to improve the accommodation for their workers.

Undated arial view of Higher Walton showing the Mill with its two chimneys and (1) the spinning block, (2) the weaving sheds, (3) All Saints Church, (4) the school, (5) the football field, (6) the Mill Tavern with Darwen Row behind, (7) Cann bridge. The River Darwen follows the line of trees from right to left. This was the layout of the village in late Victorian times.

(Photograph from the collection of Rita & John Massam)

The *'Preston Chronicle'* of 1860 made the following observations: *"Since the property has come into the possession of the Rodgetts, they have made wonderful improvements at Higher Walton. They appear to be completely remodelling and modernising the village. Old cottages are being pulled down.....to make way for good substantial habitations."* Other mill owners, such as Titus Salt in Bradford, had the vision to build model villages for their workers, providing not only accommodation but also schools, churches and other facilities.

In 1860 the new mill block was extended further, and a new chimney, boiler house, steam engine house and water tower were built. This resulted in the impressive mill profile we see today, whose cast-iron drainpipes proudly display the date of their birth.

Village life.

Anthony Hewitson visited the village in 1872 and described it as follows: *"Higher Walton stands on an eminence near the river Darwen and posesses all the characteristics of a fairly civilised and growing village, It can boast a church, a chapel, a very large manufacturing establishment, sundry public houses and beershops, two finely-named terraces – the Victoria and the Albert – good schools and one or two of Dunville's whiskey sign boards"*. He also commented on the mill which *" has about the longest chimney in this part of Christendom. For miles that chimney, about 300 feet high, can be seen"*. The mill eventually had two chimneys, one at each end of the mill, but only the smaller one remains today. Any stranger passing through the village would be closely scrutinised. Hewitson wrote:*"We turned round and saw half-a-dozen very highly-civilised Walton youths standing against a house end, and found they were discussing ...our leggings. They are good observers at Walton - everyone from the youngest to the oldest, will come out of their houses, and stand wondering and looking for half an hour if anyone passes through the village"* These inquisitive villagers became enthusiastic supporters when football arrived in the village a few years later.

Higher Walton village in 2005 showing the mill (left), the old school building (centre) and All Saints church (right). The water of Manybrooks flows from right to left in the foreground and it eventually flows into the River Darwen.   (photograph by the author)

The Church of All Saints, built in 1862, was designed by the well-known architects Austin and Paley of Lancaster. It was first built without a spire, which was added later in 1871. The Rodgetts provided the land, £1000 towards the building of the church and a peal of six bells. It was an important part of village life and was well attended. Hewitson noted that in the 1870s, *"The average attendance on a Sunday, at each service, is about 300 - principally working people."* The vicar of All Saints at this time was Rev.W.B. Shepherd. He was described as being *"white featured, red-whiskered, heavily-moustached, middle-sized and quick in his movements"*.

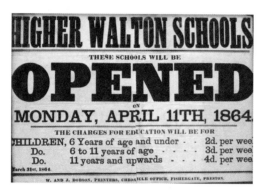

Poster advertising the opening of the first Higher Walton school. This is now displayed in the new Higher Walton C.E. Primary school which opened in 1998.

The Rodgetts also built Higher Walton Day School in 1864 for the children of the workers, and supported it financially. Edward Rodgett was a regular visitor to the school. For example, in October 1871 the Headmistress wrote: *"On Wednesday we were visited by Edward Rodgett Esquire. He took dimensions of the [school] room and promised we should have a new stove. The present one does not throw out enough heat"*.The number of children who attended school went up and down. The weather or illness could keep the pupils away. In February 1872 the infants school logbook recorded *"a great falling off of numbers of children as many were attacked by measles"* and in January 1873 *"a very thin school owing to the severity of the weather"*.

Parents had to pay a weekly fee to send their child to school and some were too poor to afford it. In January 1871 the logbook commented, *" one boy left school because of having to pay 3d per week."*

Notwithstanding these problems, the school provided a sound education, strongly founded in Christianity. The pupils were taught songs and hymns and were told Bible and other stories. The headmistress wrote in September 1871 " *On Tuesday I gave the children a lesson on 'Chalk' and on Thursday one on ' Horses'. Today I taught them a song 'the Fox' and heard them repeat their multiplication tables up to 12 times*". Some of the children were taught by a *'pupil teacher'*. This practice was quite common in Victorian times.

Village life centred on the mill, the school, the church and the local taverns. In 1877 a trade directory of Preston and District lists two inns, the *'Mill Tavern'* near the mill gates and the *'Swan Inn'*, on the hill overlooking the mill. There were also *'beerhouses'* including the *'Farmers Arms'*, near the football ground, the *'Church Tavern'* opposite the church and the *'Brookhouse Tavern'* at Manybrooks. The latter two no longer exist but the others continue to provide refreshment to the villagers.

The Dewhursts.

Following a recession in the cotton industry (the *'Cotton Famine'* of the 1860s, caused by the American Civil War), the Rodgett family decided to sell the business. In 1875 Higher Walton mills passed into the ownership of the Dewhurst family, who owned other cotton mills in the Preston area. It was one of the larger mills, eventually employing over 1000 workers, with 68,000 spindles for spinning and 1,100 looms for weaving. The Dewhurst company continued to support the village school and built the Higher Walton Institute in 1883.

The Dewhurst emblem - a wolf's head. Carved in stone, it can be seen above the door of the women's institute, built in 1922 next to the Mill Tavern.

Members could use the facilities: a games room with billiard tables, a newspaper reading room and a bathhouse for men. This building, with its stained glass windows and plaster decoration, still stands opposite the Mill Tavern and is now a café (photograph on page 76).

PRESTON

TYRE FABRIC
MANUFACTURING COMPANY LTD

CORD FABRICS
BELTING, HOSE AND TYRE

DUCKS
BRAIDING YARNS
AND
LIGHT FABRICS FOR THE
RUBBER TRADE

HIGHER WALTON MILLS, PRESTON

G & R Dewhurst Ltd. owned the mill until 1932 when it became part of the *'Lancashire Cotton Corporation'*. It remained a cotton mill until 1937 when *'Preston Tyre Fabric Ltd'* took it over to manufacture cord fabric for tyres, belting and hoses. Its life as a textile mill ended in 1977 and it is now divided into small industrial units.

Working life.

As the cotton mill expanded and prospered in the mid-1800s, so the population of the village grew. Most people were employed in the mill: the men working as overlookers, tacklers, fitters, grinders, engineers or labourers and the women as weavers, throstle spinners, warpers, winders, loomers, rovers, drawers and sizers. Children worked full-time in the mill from the age of 14. There was a high proportion of Irish workers in the village, living in the poorer housing. One such row of terraced houses was Darwen Street; often called *'Darren Row'* or *'Half-crown Row'* by the villagers. After the houses were demolished it became the car park behind the Post Office. Standing there today, you can hardly believe that sixteen terraced houses were crammed into this tiny area. According to the census of 1881 some 80 people lived here, with about half the households having Irish connections. There was also a small slaughter house in Darwen Street and in times gone by children would go there to peek through the doors with a morbid curiosity.

Although life was hard for the mill workers in late Victorian times, a change in their habits came about in the 1880s. The introduction of half-day working on Saturdays meant that the workers had the opportunity to play or watch sports on Saturday afternoons. Although traditional sports such as cricket were still popular, it was the relatively new game of *'association'* football that captured the imagination of the ordinary working man.

THE GROWTH OF ASSOCIATION FOOTBALL IN LANCASHIRE

Origins of football.

Football is an ancient game. Various forms have been played in different parts of the world for hundreds, if not thousands, of years. In England, village football was rough and unruly. This type of football is still played today in a few places such as Kirkwall in the Orkneys and Ashbourne in Derbyshire. The Ashbourne game, which is

Temporary road sign in Ashbourne. Shop windows are boarded-up as the game takes place on the streets of the town.

played every Shrove Tuesday and Ash Wednesday, involves two teams of men (the *'Up'ards'* and *'Down'ards'*) trying to get a ball to one end of the village or the other by any means possible. With one hundred players on each side, it is more like a riot than a game, but fun to watch! This type of mass football is rough and violent and can result in serious injuries. For centuries the authorities tried to stop these unruly games, and this was the main problem: there were no standardised rules for games of street or *'mob'* football.

In the early 1800s the English Public Schools were also playing games of football, with each school having its own rules. Those games were under more control and were less violent but they involved both handling and kicking a ball. It was from this background that a group of gentlemen met in London in 1863 to standardise the rules of football. The teams they represented, all from the south of England, called themselves the *'Football Association'*, shortened to *'FA.'* Differences of opinion about certain rules (such as running with the ball) led to a breakaway group who eventually formed the *'Rugby Football Association.'*

Once the rules of the *'association'* game had been decided, the FA set up an annual cup competition, the *'FA Cup'*, in 1872. The first winners were the *'Wanderers'*. They were a club from London who played at the Oval cricket ground and used guest players from other clubs. For the next ten years, until 1882, the Cup was won by teams from the south of England with ex-public school or university players, namely *'Oxford University'*, *'Royal Engineers'*, *'Old Etonians'*, *'Clapham Rovers'* and *'Old Carthusians'*. However, in 1883 the football world was turned upside down when *'Blackburn Olympic'*, a team of mill workers, beat the public school old boys' team *'Old Etonians'* in the FA Cup Final. The South's domination was over and teams from the industrial North and Midlands, in particular *'Blackburn Rovers'*, *'Preston North End'* and *'West Bromwich Albion'*, rose to prominence. The *'Lancashire FA'* had been formed in 1878 and the Lancashire Cup competition started in 1879.

Football spreads.

Many teams had their origins in the local church or factory. For example, Bolton Wanderers started as *'Christ Church'* in 1874, Everton started as *'St Domingo's Church'* in 1878 and West Bromwich Albion was formed by employees of Salter's spring works in 1878. In 1882, Higher Walton also formed a village team, using local players who were mainly mill workers. In its early seasons it played against local opposition but within a few years it had become such a force that the *'Villagers'*, as the team was known, were playing against leading clubs such as Blackburn Rovers, Everton, Bolton, Blackpool, Burnley and Bury. Its rise was meteoric but its fall was just as rapid, and by 1893 it was again a small village team playing in the Preston leagues.

The area of Lancashire around Blackburn, Darwen, Bolton, and Preston was the heart of the cotton industry and football was first played there in the 1870s. Blackburn Rovers was formed by a group of ex-public schoolboys in 1875. Preston North End was originally formed as a cricket club in 1865, but in 1878 played its first game of association football, against Eagley.

Although there was the prestigious FA Cup to enter each season, teams did not play in leagues as they do today. A series of friendly fixtures called *'club'* games would be arranged. Darwen would play Blackburn Rovers, Blackburn Olympic would play Preston North End and so on. The first league, the *'Football League'*, did not start until 1888.

Football was also well established in Scotland and the leading Scottish teams were permitted to enter the English FA Cup. The top northern teams arranged regular friendlies against Scottish teams. This not only added a little spice to the fixture list but good Scottish players were easily spotted. It was not long before teams in the North West, such as Preston North End and Blackburn Rovers began to sign these players, with the promise of a better job in the local mill as an incentive. Paying players was illegal until 1885 because the Football Association rules insisted on amateur status. However, there is no doubt that some players were paid to play and this latent professionalism (*'shamateurism'*) was one of the reasons why football teams of the Lancashire cotton towns began to dominate English football in the 1880s.

The rules of the game.

During the 1870s the basic rules of association football had been laid down by the FA. The game was eleven-a-side, played on a pitch with similar dimensions to the present day but with very few markings other than the touch lines. Throw-ins were one-handed in the 1870s but two-handed in the 1880s. There were no penalty kicks, only free kicks. Goalkeepers could handle the ball anywhere on the pitch. Before the turn of the century, goalkeepers were fair game and could be charged whether they had the ball or not! The game was certainly rougher than today. The offside rule was similar to modern football, except three players, rather than two, had to be between player and goal. The goalposts were 8 yards apart and 8 feet high, exactly the same as today. In 1875 the crossbar was introduced to replace a piece of tape across the top of the posts, which had been the cause of some disputed goals. The goals had no nets until 1892.

From the early days in the 1870s the game was controlled by two *'umpires'*, one from each team, and a *'referee'* to resolve any disputes. This system had its origins in cricket. The umpires each patrolled half of the pitch, and carried a stick or flag. If an incident occurred, a player could appeal and the umpire would raise his flag if he agreed with the appeal. If both umpires raised their flags then the referee was not needed, but if only one umpire raised his flag the referee would be called on to make the final decision. The referee was there chiefly as a timekeeper but he could also arbitrate if the umpires disagreed. This system underwent a major change in 1891 when the referee took full control of the game and the umpires moved to the touchlines to become *'linesmen'*. The referee or umpire could blow a whistle to stop the game and these were being used as early as 1872.

Kitted out.

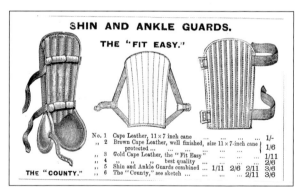

Advertisements taken from Granville's 1892 sports catalogue.
(National Football Museum collection)

SHIN AND ANKLE GUARDS.

THE "FIT EASY."

THE "COUNTY."

No. 1	Cape Leather, 11 × 7 inch cane	1/-
,, 2	Brown Cape Leather, well finished, size 11 × 7-inch cane protected	1/6
,, 3	Gold Cape Leather, the " Fit Easy "	1/11
,, 4	,, ,, ,, best quality	2/6
,, 5	Shin and Ankle Guards combined ... 1/11 2/6 2/11	3/6
,, 6	The "County," see sketch ... 2/11	3/6

In the early days players wore either long trousers (*'knickerbockers'* or *'breeches'*) or knee-length shorts (*'knicks'*), often held up with a belt. The shirt was made of wool or cotton. Goalkeepers had the same coloured shirt as the rest of the team and often wore gloves. Shinguards had been invented in 1874 by Sam Widdowson who adapted the pads used in cricket. Before 1900 they were worn *outside* the socks.

The "Embee" Button End or Capless Ball.
9.6 EACH, THREE FOR 27/-, POST FREE.

The leather ball was much the same size and weight as it is today but had a rubber inner bladder and was laced up. It was made out of panels (like the segments of an orange), sometimes with buttons at the end. Unlike modern footballs, which have a plastic coating to make them waterproof, the old leather balls soon lost their water resistance. They became very wet and heavy - hence the belief that footballs were much heavier in those days, when in fact the official size and dry weight of the ball has hardly changed in the past 100 years.

At first virtually any type of boot was worn for a game of football, though metal spikes on the sole were banned. However, maufacturers soon began to produce special football boots with leather studs or bars underneath for extra grip. They realised that there was money to be made out of the new sport and produced an ever-increasing amount

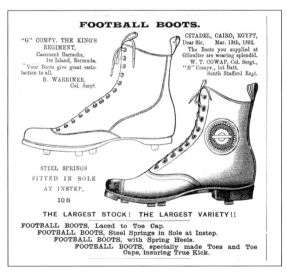

FOOTBALL BOOTS.

"G" COMPY. THE KING'S REGIMENT,
Casement Barracks,
Ire Island, Bermuda.
"Your Boots give great satisfaction to all.
B. WARRINER,
Col. Sergt.

CITADEL, CAIRO, EGYPT,
Dear Sir,   Mar. 13th, 1892.
The Boots you supplied at Gibraltar are wearing splendid.
W. T. COWAP, Col. Sergt.,
"B" Compy., 1st Batt.
South Stafford Regt.

STEEL SPRINGS
FITTED IN SOLE
AT INSTEP,
10.6

THE LARGEST STOCK! THE LARGEST VARIETY!!

FOOTBALL BOOTS, Laced to Toe Cap.
  FOOTBALL BOOTS, Steel Springs in Sole at Instep.
    FOOTBALL BOOTS, with Spring Heels.
      FOOTBALL BOOTS, specially made Toes and Toe Caps, insuring True Kick.

of football kit, equipment, boots and balls. By the 1880s, sports outfitters such as Piggotts, Lillywhites and Gamages were advertising widely in magazines. Football was rapidly becoming the most popular sport in Britain and Lancashire was at the very heart of this revolution.

FOOTBALL ARRIVES IN HIGHER WALTON (1882-85)

The first *'Higher Walton Football Club'* was formed in 1882 and was based at the *'Mill Tavern'* on Cann Bridge Street. Their Secretary was William Harwood who lived at number 1, Victoria Terrace. This row of terraced houses lies directly opposite the *'Farmers Arms'* public house and is now numbered 331 to 347 Higher Walton Road. To the rear of these houses is the field, now called *'King George V playing field'*, where the team probably played its home games. William, who was 45 years old, worked at the mill as a cotton overlooker and had eight children. Two of his children, Thomas and Alfred, were probably the T. Harwood and A. Harwood who played for the team in 1885. The team soon became referred to by the nicknames *'Moon's Mill'*, the *'Waltonians'* or simply the *'Villagers'*.

During their first season (1882-83) the team did not enter the FA Cup or Lancashire Cup because they were not yet affiliated to the Lancashire Football Association. Fixtures were all *'club'* games, because no leagues existed before 1888. They arranged fixtures against local teams; Brownedge, School Lane (Bamber Bridge), Walton-le-Dale, Lostock Hall, Brindle, Preston Swifts, Preston Rangers, Fishwick Ramblers, Croston, Heapy, Darwen Old Wanderers, St Thomas's (Blackburn) and Parish Church (Preston). Many of these teams had only been in existance a short time.

Kick off.

The first game recorded in local newspapers was played on the 30th September 1882 when Higher Walton defeated Lostock Hall 3-1. The following Saturday they had another home fixture against Brindle which they won 4-0. According to the *'Preston Guardian'* the game was *"watched by a considerable number of spectators"*. The *'Preston Herald'* reported *"The Brindle team was strengthened by three from Witton but the excellent passing of the home team completely baffled the Brindle backs"*. In the early days of football, *'old boys'* teams such as the Wanderers would play a dribbling game in which the main tactic of the forwards was to dribble the ball up the field to score.

16

Teams had a formation of goalkeeper, one fullback, two half-backs and seven forwards! However, a passing game was favoured by Scottish and Northern teams and this soon proved to be more effective. The players then lined up in a manner that continued well into the twentieth century. In front of the goalkeeper were two full backs (right and left), three half backs (right, centre and left) and five forwards (right winger, inside right, centre, forward, inside left and left winger). By the 1880s it was generally agreed that good 'combination', that is play which involved passing and movement, was more successful than individual dribbling.

On 14th October Higher Walton lost 4-2 to their local rivals, School Lane. At that time School Lane was very much a separate community and not just part of Bamber Bridge, as it is today. The game was *"played at the Higher Walton ground in front of 400 spectators and the match ball was presented by Mr Tom Sharp of Higher Walton"*. The return match was played on 13th January 1883 and, according to the *'Preston Guardian'*, the field was in a wretched condition and although Higher Walton played well they were unable to score more than one goal *"on account of a large puddle in front of the goal"*! To make matters worse they scored two own goals and lost 2-1. We know the full team for this game which was *J. Harrison (goal), Stott and Phelan (backs), T. Coulston, Law, Naylor (half-backs), W. Coulston, Iddon, T. Naylor, Roscoe, G. Coulston (forwards)*. The three Coulstons were probably the sons of William Coulston, a grocer of Kittlingborne Brow who was the Parish Clerk and lived at 2, Adamson's Row. William (aged 26) and George (aged 19) were railway clerks and Thomas (aged 17) was an apprentice joiner. By 1895 William junior had become the village butcher at 11, Cann Bridge Street, where Ken Bamber's butcher's shop is today.

The names Iddon and Naylor would feature strongly in the great Higher Walton team of a few years later.

On 3rd March 1883, Higher Walton beat Brownedge 4-1 in front of 500 spectators and, according to the newspapers, they played *"a grand passing game"*. By the end of their first season Higher Walton had played at least 22 games, winning 10, drawing 3 and losing 9. They also ran a second (reserve) team.

Travels in Lancashire.

In their second season (1883-84) Higher Walton arranged fixtures against teams a little further afield. These included Wesham (Kirkham), Ribchester, Low Moor (Clitheroe), Darwen Hibernians, Preston Swifts, Oswaldtwistle Rovers, Blackburn Park Road, Darwen St John's, Peel Park (Accrington), Darwen 'A' team, Bamber Bridge, Blackburn Olympic Reserves and Blackburn Perseverance.

On 8th September 1883 Higher Walton drew 3-3 with Darwen Old Wanderers at home, with a team almost identical to the one that had played School Lane in January, apart from Winter who replaced Roscoe. On 15th September they travelled to Blackburn to play Blackburn Olympic's second team. Olympic's first team had just caused a major shock by beating Old Etonians 2-1 in the English Cup final. They were the first *'working class'* team from the North of England to win the Cup. Their reserve team was also very good and they thrashed Higher Walton 9-2. Olympic's success was short-lived and they were soon replaced by Blackburn Rovers as the premier team in Blackburn.

Higher Walton was now registered with the Lancashire FA and entered the Lancashire Cup for the first time. The competition had started five years earlier and for the 1883-84 season the competition attracted an entry of 84 teams from all over Lancashire. Before league football was introduced, this competition was taken seriously by the bigger Lancashire Clubs such as Blackburn Rovers and Preston North End , and was second only to the FA Cup in prestige.

On 20th October 1883 Higher Walton easily beat Oswaldtwistle St Paul's 8-3 in the first round and the team was *Harrison, Holt, Phelan, Law, T.Coulston, Lee, G.Coulston, Naylor, J.Winter, W.Coulston, Iddon.* St Paul's appealed and the game had to be replayed. It was quite common in those days for the losing team in a cup game to appeal against the result on the grounds of ineligible players or pitch size. Higher Walton won the replay 3-0 but in the second round they lost 5-2 at Loveclough (Rossendale), putting an end to their first cup run.

One of Higher Walton's players (Tom Naylor) had broken a leg in December so a benefit game was played against Bamber Bridge on 12th January. Higher Walton won 4-0 in front of 500 spectators. A broken leg meant the player would not be able to work in the mill, so the money collected at the benefit game would have been given to Tom and his family.

On 26th January 1884 Higher Walton played at the famous *'Barley Bank'* ground of Darwen FC against their 'A' team. Darwen were one of the strongest Lancashire teams in the late 1870s and in 1879 they took the famous Old Etonians to a second replay in the FA Cup. They were probably the first Lancashire team to sign professional players: Scotsmen Fergie Suter and James Love. In 1881 Darwen reached the semi-final of the FA Cup. Local rivalry with Blackburn Rovers resulted in several acrimonious games between the two teams and rival supporters often caused trouble. The 1884 game involving Higher Walton and Darwen's reserve team was never completed for a different reason. It was abandoned with Higher Walton leading 1-0, *"owing to the wet and boisterous weather"*. The Higher Walton team was *T.Lee, Phelan, Osbaldeston, T.Coulston, Lee, Moran, W.Coulston, Iddon, G.Coulston, Crook, Winter.*

On 8th March Higher Walton played host to Low Moor of Clitheroe. The *'Preston Herald'* stated: *"The ground was in capital order and the weather fine.The whole village turned out to salute the Lower Moor team: nearly 1000 spectators were assembled. The visitors arrived late and the game kicked off at 4pm"*. The final result was a 5-2 win for Low Moor.

A late kick-off was quite common in those days because the players had finished work at one o'clock then had to travel by train then horse-drawn wagonette to the away ground. If we can believe the attendance figures given in the newspapers, spectators were often numbered in the hundreds or thousands, indicating the rapid growth in popularity of football as a spectator sport. Higher Walton's final record for 1883-4 was played 24, won 15, drawn 2, lost 7, goals for 72, against 51.

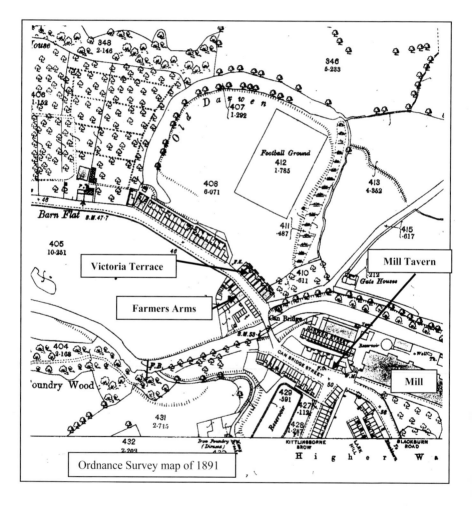

Ordnance Survey map of 1891

Home ground.

Higher Walton probably played their home games on the field that is now known as *'King George V playing fields'*. They were definitely playing there in 1891 because the pitch appears on the 2 inch to a mile Ordnance Survey map of Higher Walton. One feature to catch the eye on this map is the loop of water round the field: the old route of the River Darwen. In much earlier times the river had developed a hugh meandering loop, which was eventually cut off to form what is called an *'oxbow lake'*. The football field was in the centre of an *'island'* bounded by water or marshy land. No doubt this caused a problem when the ball landed in it, but a net on a pole was a likely solution. There are tales of unpopular referees being thrown into this river at the end of a game, though these should be taken with a pinch of salt.

The pitch measured about 115 yards by 75 yards (1.8 acres) but there was never any permanent terracing or covered stand built for spectators. They would simply stand around the edge of the pitch, with possibly a rope as an enclosure. For big games, wagons may have been drawn onto the field to act as temporary stands. The hill at the north end of the ground, called *'Billy Brows'*, may also have been a good vantage point for some spectatators, though it was the other side of the *'Old Darwen'*. In those early years the team did not change at the ground but used the Mill Tavern and then walked over Cann (or *'Can'*) bridge to the pitch. There were other football teams playing around the village at this time. Newspapers recorded results for Higher Walton Ramblers, Higher Walton Grasshoppers, Higher Walton Stars and Higher Walton Hill Climbers, but these teams were short-lived.

Local derbies.

For the 1884-85 season Higher Walton's colours were recorded in *'The Football Annual'* as *"blue and white halves"*, similar to Blackburn Rovers. Their secretary was still William Harwood and *"Mr R.Iddon"* of Higher Walton was on the committee of the Lancashire F.A.

This was probably Richard Iddon, aged 48, a mill engineer who lived in the village. He was voted onto the Lancashire FA Executive Committee in 1884 as one of the two Preston District representatives, along with the famous Major William Sudell of Preston North End. Richard Iddon remained on the Lancashire FA committee until 1894, then from 1895 to 1901 he served as vice president. No doubt he played a major part in the rise of Higher Walton as a footballing force.

This season the team had fixtures against School Lane, Witton, Rishton, Greenwood Millers, Darwen Old Wanderers, Peel Bank Rovers of Church, Fishwich Ramblers, Preston Swifts, Low Moor, Blackpool St John's, Oswaldtwistle Rovers, Bell's Temperance of Accrington, Lostock Hall and Preston Zingari. Games against School Lane were big derby matches and crowds of between 500 and 800 spectators were commonplace. Higher Walton entered the FA Cup for the first time but lost 4-1 at Darwen Old Wanderers in the first round. In the first round of the Lancashire Cup they beat Kearsley 11-0 but lost 5-2 to Darcy Lever in the second round in November 1884. Higher Walton played a club game against Preston Swifts on 31st January 1885. At half time the Swifts were 2-1 ahead but early in the second half *"a good shot was sent in by Winter and caught by Saunders, who was sent through the posts by Iddon to make the game equal"*. Charging the goalkeeper through the posts when he was holding the ball was allowed. The winning goal was scored by Winter *"putting it through the posts amidst great cheering."* Higher Walton had won 3-2. Note that the goals had no nets until 1892.

On 14th February 1885 the 'Villagers' travelled to Clitheroe and drew 2-2 with Low Moor. The team that day was *T. Coulston, Osbaldeston, Daley, Cook, Lee, Harwood, Wilson, Naylor, Iddon, Doyle, Winter.* The following week they defeated Blackpool St John's 5-3. This club was a predecessor of the present day Blackpool FC.

An interesting comment appeared in the *'Preston Herald'* that week. *"The Fishwick Ramblers met South Shore at Blackpool.... One of the Ramblers players was very seriously injured and had to be carried off the field. Dr Richardson said he had one of his ribs broken....There are complaints all round as to the rough play generally resorted to by the Blackpool and South Shore Clubs. The injury was caused by an 'elbow charge', a most reprehensible mode of charging. Surely the seaside clubs must be aware that brutal play is not in any sense football".* Although the game in those days was rougher and the goalkeeper could be charged, only *'fair'* charges were allowed. This is an early example of the football rivalry that still exists between Preston and Blackpool.

In April 1885 Higher Walton played a local derby at Lostock Hall in front of 500 spectators. Teams could play guest players and Jack Yates of Blackburn Olympic played for Higher Walton. He was a positive and forceful outside left. In the derby game, according to the press, he was *"bottled up"* by the Lostock Hall defence and Higher Walton lost 3-1. Jack later played for Accrington and Burnley in the Football League and won one England cap in 1889 against  Ireland. He scored a hat-trick but was never selected again! Higher Walton's next game (a 1-1 draw) was against Preston North End's reserve team, a sure sign that they were looking for opponents of a higher standard. Their record for the 1884-85 season was: played 29 games, won 12, drawn 8, lost 8, goals for 64 and against 47.

Professional or amateur?
The national controversy over professionalism came to a head in 1885. The Football Association opposed the payment of players but a number of northern Clubs, led by Preston North End's William Sudell, wanted to legalise these payments. Some Clubs even threatened to form a break-away football association for northern clubs. In January a special meeting was held in London to attempt to change the rules and Higher Walton sent a delegate. A majority of clubs were in favour of professionalism and later in the year the FA reluctantly allowed professional football but under strict rules.

Higher Walton probably supported this move, even though they were only a small club. Many football clubs, including Higher Walton, were charging admission for spectators, and it seemed logical to pay the players. This would prove to be the eventual downfall of the first Higher Walton club.

For the 1885-86 season new opponents included Livesey Grasshoppers, South Shore of Blackpool, Chorley and Kirkham. One most interesting fixture took place on 10th October against Bootle. They were one of the leading clubs in Liverpool, second only to Everton. Liverpool Football Club was yet to be formed. Although Higher Walton lost 4-2, it was an indication that that they were

willing to challenge the better teams in Lancashire. The cup games in this season proved to be a disappointment, as they lost 3-4 to South Shore in the first round of the FA Cup and lost 5-1 to Park Road (Blackburn) in the Lancashire Senior Cup. The number of entries for the Lancashire Cup exceeded 100, so two competitions were run, the Senior and Junior Cups. The team in that game was *Coulston, Osbaldeston, Daley, A. Harwood, Leigh, Wood, T. Harwood, Wilson, Baldwin, Halstead, Naylor*. The two Harwoods were probably Thomas (aged 21) and Alfred (aged 19), sons of secretary William Harwood.

The Lancashire
Senior Cup

Although substitutes were not allowed in games, when Higher Walton played Fishwick Ramblers one of their players had to retire hurt but *"by kind permission of the home captain a substitute was allowed to take his place"*. This gentlemanly conduct did not extend to all games. Against Preston Swifts, in January 1886, Higher Walton were not happy with the second goal scored against them and left the field as a protest before the end of the game. They never played the Swifts again. The *'Preston Herald'* also noted: *"The visitors [Higher Walton] wore mourning for the late patron of the club, Mr Rodgett"*. This is a reference to Edward Rodgett, the previous mill owner.

RISE TO GREATNESS (1886-88)

In the 1886-7 season Higher Walton became more adventurous in their travels, with fixtures against Fleetwood Rangers, Rishton, Livesey Grasshoppers, South Shore, Low Moor, Bell's Temperance (of Accrington), Blackpool, Wigan and Adlington, in addition to local games against Cherry Tree, Fishwick Ramblers, Chorley, Lostock Hall and St Joseph's (Preston). In the first round of the Lancashire Senior Cup, Higher Walton were drawn away to Fishwick Ramblers. The game was played at *'Fishwick Brow'* on 25th September 1886 in front of 500 spectators in wet weather and the Waltonians played *"some grand football"*. They charged into a 4-0 lead, before a late fight back by the Ramblers brought the score back to 4-3 at the final whistle. Higher Walton's team was *Collins, Sharples, Daley, Rose, Ward, Coulston, Doyle, Iddon, Mather, Jackson, Naylor.* Several of these players *(Collins, Daley, Rose, Iddon, Mather and Naylor)* were to be key players in the successful team of later years. William Henry *('Billy')* Mather was the 20 year-old son of John Mather, the landlord of the *'Farmers Arms'* beerhouse in Higher Walton.

Scottish adventure.

The FA Cup brought a more challenging fixture for Higher Walton. They were drawn away to a Scottish team, Third Lanark of Glasgow. Scottish teams were permitted to enter the English Cup, but this was to be the last season that this was allowed. Queen's Park of Glasgow had even reached the Cup Final in 1884 and 1885 but had been beaten by Blackburn Rovers on both occasions. Third Lanark, or *'Third Lanarkshire Rifle Volunteers'* as they were originally called, were also tough opponents. They were one of the top Scottish teams who regularly provided players for the international team and would soon win the Scottish Cup (in 1889). They played their games at *'Cathkin Park'* in Glasgow, which had been used for international games. *"Several thousand"* spectators watched the game on 16th October 1886 and in a one-sided first half Higher Walton conceded five goals.

The second half was more even and the game ended in a 5-0 defeat for Higher Walton. The newspapers were somewhat critical of the English opposition. *"The Waltonians never tested the abilities of the Volunteers, who simply did as they pleased in a careless way in the second half"*. The Higher Walton team was: *Joseph Collins, T.Sharples, T.Daley, Robert Ward, W. Ross, T. Coulston, J. Doyle, Billy Mather, W.Jackson, T.Naylor, T.Iddon,.* The latter was possibly Thomas Iddon, aged 19, a mill engine fitter and son of Richard Iddon senior.

Th' Owd Reds.

England cap won by 'Jud' Haworth. In purple velvet, this design, with the English rose, was used until 1938 when the *'three lions'* badge was adopted. (photographed with permission of the National Football Museum)

In the next round of the Lancashire Cup, Higher Walton were drawn at home to a top team, *'Accrington FC'*, who would become one of the founder members of the Football League in the following season. Accrington would remain in the Football League for 5 seasons before being relegated and disbanded in 1895. They should not be confused with *'Accrington Stanley'*, a different club, which entered the Football League in the 1920s. The Cup game was played on 6th November 1886 and a large crowd of about 1000 watched the game against *"Th' Owd Reds"* as they became known. The Accrington team contained George (*'Jud'*) Howarth, a hard-tackling half-back who won five international caps for England between 1887 and 1890. The *'Waltonians'* fought with great determination but the match ended in a 6-1 victory for Accrington. Doyle scored Higher Walton's only goal and Jack Yates, once a guest player for Higher Walton, scored one of the Accrington goals. The *'Villagers'* team was *Collins, Daley, Rose, Ward, Sharples, Coulston, Iddon, Doyle, Mather, Jackson, Naylor.* Although Higher Walton were outclassed in the cup games, they performed well in club games, and their record for the season was played 32, won 25, drawn 1, lost 6, goals for 110, goals against 51.

Scores of 8-2 against Rishton, 10-0 against Adlington and 6-0 against Livesey Grasshoppers were some of the highlights of this season. One game, in March 1887, against Fishwick Ramblers, was a benefit game for Tom Coulston who was going to Australia. Ward and Doyle also retired from the game at the end of the season. The excellent goalkeeper, Joseph Collins, had left half way through the season to play in Scotland but he was replaced by an equally good 'keeper called Chapman.

The 1887-8 season began with the good news in the *'Preston Herald'* that *"the best players of last season, Chapman, Daly, Rose, Baldwin, Iddon, Mather and Naylor are all available"*. The team's colours were now given as *"chocolate, blue and white"* in *'The Football Annual'*. We could perhaps envisage shirts with brown and light blue stripes and white shorts. The first home game was against Padiham on 17th September and the newspapers reported a strange incident during the 2-0 win. *"This being the first match at home a large number of spectators assembled. Iddon headed the ball through [the posts] from a pass by Blackburn. This was disallowed, the visitors alleging that the ball had burst before it went through"*. The ball has to be a standard size throughout the game so this was a correct decision, but it was a little bizarre. The following week, Higher Walton played Wigan who were totally outclassed. According to the match report, *"By the second half the visitors were run off their feet and soon after the home team had increased the lead to 12, the visitor's umpire left the field, not being able to agree with the referee's decision."* Chapman in goal was *"exceedingly cool"* and the final score was 13-1 to Higher Walton.

Up for t'Cup.

Higher Walton made good progress in both cup competitions. In the first round of the Lancashire Senior Cup they were drawn at home to Halliwell, from Bolton, who were a team of similar quality to Bolton Wanderers. Higher Walton won the game 3-2, which surprised many commentators. During the game a Higher Walton player was injured: *"Blackburn was hurt through Lucas jumping on him"* Ouch!

In the second round (19th November 1887), they were again drawn at home against their old rivals, Accrington. A reported crowd of 4000, probably the biggest ever to assemble at Higher Walton, saw Accrington go into a 4-goal lead by half time. The second half was more even and the game ended in a 4-0 win to Accrington. The newspapers commented that the Football League professionals were probably better in front of goal: in other words they were better at finishing. This was the second year running that Accrington had proved to be too much for the village team, and it would not be the last.

In the FA Cup Higher Walton got as far as the third round. In the first round (15th October) they were due to play Heywood Central at home but when the opposition arrived they announced that they had *"scratched"*, that is conceded the game. A friendly was played instead which the Waltonians won 8-1. This was the very day that Preston North End were recording their record 26-0 Cup win against Hyde. In the second round on 5th November 1887, Higher Walton played Fleetwood Rangers and a special train was chartered to take supporters to the coast. Higher Walton ran out 3-1 winners in front of 3000 spectators.

They were rewarded by a trip to Bootle in the third round on 26th November 1887. The team now included full back Jack Mather, the younger brother of Billy Mather, the centre forward. Jack was moved to right wing in later games. The full team that day was *Chapman, J.Mather, T.Daly, J.Baldwin, T.Coulston, W.Rose, W.Jackson, T.Iddon, W.Mather, Naylor, Blackburn*. Bootle again proved to be too strong for the *'Villagers'*.

The 'Bootle Times' said "Throughout the first half Walton played a purely defensive game, rarely venturing an attack" and by half time the score was 4-0 to Bootle. In the second half, "Walton plucked up and played better but were unable to make headway against the superior combination of their opponents". An incident occurred in the second half in which "J. Mather and Anderson deliberately handled the ball, and a scuffle ensued in which Anderson was winded". This would not be the last time Jack Mather would get involved in a 'punch up' on the field! Higher Walton's goalkeeper, Chapman, was praised for keeping the score down but the final result was 6-1 to Bootle.

Higher Walton again did well in ordinary club games beating teams such as Haydock, Padiham, Fishwick Ramblers, St Joseph's, Lostock Hall, Lower Darwen, Lower House, Chorley, South Shore, Oswaldtwistle Rovers and Fleetwood Rangers. In fact they remained undefeated at home, apart from the cup game. The season's record was: played 31, won 21, drawn 5, lost 6, goals for 125, against 50.

THE FARMERS ARMS public house in Higher Walton in the early 1880s.
The two people are probably John Mather, the father of footballers Billy and Jack Mather, and Elizabeth their sister. She became the licensee after John died in 1888.
(photograph supplied by the late Harry Mather)

29

For the 1888-89 season, Richard Iddon (junior) took over as Secretary. He was probably the 29 year old mill book keeper and the son of Richard Iddon senior. The club colours were still chocolate, blue & white. The team's record in all matches was excellent (played 37, won 26, drawn 5, lost 6, goals for 99, against 54) and in the cup competitions Higher Walton really excelled. Higher Walton progressed to the fourth preliminary round of the FA Cup. Following a bye in the first round, they beat Clitheroe 7-0 in the second round, then Rossendale 3-2 in the third round before losing 5-1 to South Shore (Blackpool) in the fourth round.

Bring on the Rovers.

In the Lancashire Senior Cup, Higher Walton beat Blackburn Olympic 2-1 in the first round. Olympic were no longer the force they had been in the early 1880s. Rossendale were then defeated in the second round (2-1). In the third round, on 5th January 1889, they were drawn at home to the mighty Blackburn Rovers. Bigger clubs often fielded a weak team in the early rounds of the Lancashire Cup, leaving the big guns for the final. Rovers obviously thought that they could easily beat Higher Walton and they fielded mainly reserve players. The Higher Walton team was: *Chapman, W.Rose, T.Daley, T.Naylor, R.Spencer, J.Baldwin, J.Mather, W.Mather, T.Iddon, E. Naylor, T.Naylor.*

The Blackburn Rovers team that day was *Suter, Beverley, Barton, Holman, Wareing, Fletcher, Porter, Haresnape, Fecitt, Duerden, Blenhem.* It is interesting to note that *'Fergie'* Suter, in goal, was the famous Scottish full-back who was one of the first (illegal) professionals to play for Darwen and Blackburn. He was a stonemason who was never seen working on a piece of stone in Lancashire: he said the stone was too hard! Another famous player was Herbert *('Harry')* Fecitt, a *"dashing inside forward"* who had won two FA Cup winners' medals (in 1885 and 1886) and Joe Beverley, a fine full back, who had won one FA Cup winners medal and three England caps in 1882. The Rovers team who faced the village team should have been good enough to win, but things did not quite work out that way.

Nearly 2000 spectators lined *'the enclosure'* when Higher Walton kicked off. The first half was a rip-roaring cup match with both teams having chances: *"Fecitt sent in three scorching shots in succession"* for Rovers and Jack Mather of Higher Walton had some great shots at goal. He hit the bar then he *"levelled a stinger at Suter.... who coolly threw it away"*. By half time Higher Walton had gone into a 2-0 lead but *"the ground was visited by a dense fog"* which must have reduced the visibility for the spectators.

In the second half Rovers bombarded the Higher Walton goal, but both sides had their chances. Rovers then scored two quick goals to draw level, but, *"enlivened by the cries of their supporters"*, Higher Walton scored a third goal to take the lead. Then Walton nearly scored a fourth but this was disallowed due to handball. Rovers managed to bring the scores level at 3-3 before full time was called. Extra time could not be played because of the fog, so a replay was scheduled for 23rd February 1889.

BLACKBURN ROVERS 1889, FA Cup semi-finalists.
Players only, back row: James Southworth, H.Arthur, J.Forbes, W.Townley.
Middle row: J.Douglas, N.Walton, W.Almond, J.Forrest.
Front row: R.Haresnape, Jack Southworth (captain), H.Fecitt.

(Reproduced with permission of the National Football Museum)

31

Rovers return.

The replay took place in front of about 4,000 spectators at Blackburn Rovers' Leamington Road ground. This was their home from 1881 until 1890 when they moved to Ewood Park. The Rovers took the fixture very seriously and fielded most of their usual first team. However, three star players were absent: Jack Southworth and William Townley were away playing for England, and John Forbes was ineligible. The Rovers team was: *Herbie Arthur (goal), James Southworth, James Douglas (backs), John Barton, William Almond, James Forrest (halfbacks), Robert Haresnape, Nathanial Walton, James Beresford,, Harry Fecitt, James Duerden (forwards)*. A similar Blackburn team reached the semi-final of the FA Cup later that season and contained some great players.

Herbie Arthur wearing a Lancashire FA cap

'Herbie' Arthur was Rovers' first choice 'keeper throughout the 1880s. He won three FA Cup winners medals and seven England caps. According to Mike Jackman: *"There was little flamboyance about his style, he preferred to use positional play rather than spectacular leaps"*. In 1891 he had the distinction of playing the whole Burnley team on his own, as the rest of the Rovers team left the field during a snowstorm! Herbie successfully appealed for offside and then delayed taking the free kick so long that the referee was forced to abandon the game.

James Forrest was a key playmaker for the Rovers and holds the record for winning the most FA Cup winners medals (five). John Barton played once for England (in 1889), won two FA Cup winners' medals and eventually became the trainer at Preston North End. Jimmy Douglas was one of the Scottish players who helped Rovers to win three consecutive Cup Finals from 1884 to 1886. He was a tough little character, very skilful, but he weighed only eight stone. He started as a nippy forward but later played in defence. James Southworth was Jack Southworth's brother. He was a good professional sprinter and eventually emigrated to Australia.

On paper the Rovers team should have won easily, but the Higher Walton players were not over-awed by the reputation of the Rovers' players and were determined to give them a run for their money. The Higher Walton team was unchanged from the first game.

Rovers won the toss and decided to play with the wind. They could not have had a better start for after three minutes a cross from Nat Walton (of Rovers) was headed into the goal by Harry Fecitt. Rovers kept up the pressure and soon Fecitt scored again. James Duerden then made the score three-nil with Higher Walton appealing unsuccessfully for offside. However, with a few minutes to go to half time, a splendid centre from the left was converted into a goal by Tommy Iddon. Higher Walton were back in the game! In the second half Rovers had several chances to score but their shooting was careless. Higher Walton continued to work hard and scored two more goals, bringing the scores level. Rovers failed to respond to this shock and the *'Villagers'* scored another goal to go into a 4-3 lead. Rovers then settled down to some good play and equalised, but Higher Walton scored a fifth from a free kick. Rovers tried to equalise but ran out of time and were beaten 5-4. What a comeback by the *'Villagers'* and what a game!

The local papers were highly critical and accused the Rovers of complacency and lack of desire to win. The *'Preston Herald'* said, *"The visitors deserve every credit for their victory, for it was secured by down right energy and determination, and by gamely sticking to their work with such odds against them. The Rovers deserve and will get no sympathy. They held their opponents too cheap"*. One jubilant supporter from Higher Walton said a *"skoo"* team (meaning a *"school"* team) had beaten the Rovers. The *'Lancashire Daily Post'* observed, *"When the Rovers had run up a score of three goals to nothing it looked as if the promised thrashing would be given to the Waltonians but the ground rang with laughter when the visitors equalised. The fun grew fast and furious when they put on the leading point and Rovers made frantic efforts to avoid defeat."* The general verdict on the Rovers was that *"it served them right"*.

Toffees chewed up!

In the semi-final of the Lancashire Cup, Higher Walton were drawn against another Football League team, Everton. The game was again played at the Leamington ground in Blackburn on 16th March 1889 before *"a large number of spectators"*. The weather was poor and *"a constant drizzle lessened the enjoyment of the spectators"*. Higher Walton were unchanged from the team that beat Blackburn Rovers in February. Everton had Bob Smalley in goal. He had played against

Edgar Chadwick

Higher Walton a few years earlier for Lostock Hall, and played a total of 36 games for Everton between 1888 and 1890. Everton had several other talented players, including Edgar Chadwick who would play seven times for England between 1891 and 1896. The Everton team was *Smalley, A. Chadwick, Dobson, Sayer, Holt, Farmer, Briscoe, Fleming, Brown, E.Chadwick, Costley.* Higher Walton attacked Everton from the start and went into a two-goal lead through Jack Mather

and Tom Naylor. In the second half two Everton players had to leave the field injured and, with no substitutes being allowed, Everton were fighting an uphill battle. Eventually Edgar Chadwick scored a goal for the *"Toffeemen"* but Jack Mather then scored a third for Higher Walton and Everton were well beaten. The press said *"For the winners, Chapman the custodian, played a splendid game, and the rest of the team were very well combined, their forwards making a capital exhibition of their shooting powers ...... their victory was very well earned"*. The 'Lancashire Daily Post' commented that not only did the team have the best of the play but the Higher Walton supporters also had the best of the bad language!

Irish adventure.

The final of the Lancashire Cup was to be played on 27th April and Higher Walton's opponents were to be their old rivals Accrington, who had been very lucky to beat Haydock in the other semi-final.

The week before this vital match Higher Walton travelled to Ireland to play Distillery FC of Belfast in an Easter Festival of Football.

Advertisement in the 'Ulster Cyclist and Football News' (Belfast), 19th April 1889.

The Ulster press said *"Higher Walton brought a big lot of footballers to Broadway on Saturday. The visitors arrived with a big reputation, having defeated several of the crack clubs of Lancashire".*

The *'Villagers'* played the first half against a strong wind and defended well. Reports in the newspapers complimented them on their defensive headers, the excellent saves made by Chapman and for *"playing a nice passing game"* in attack. Higher Walton missed several chances to score in the second half but eventually a goal by Tom Naylor and an own goal gave Higher Walton a 2-0 victory. Interestingly, Distillery played another game on Easter Monday against Glasgow Celtic, and only lost 1-0.

Lancashire Cup final.

The following Saturday (27th April), Higher Walton were back in England playing in the final of the Lancashire Cup in front of 3000 spectators at the Leamington Road ground in Blackburn. There was a strong contingent of Waltonians and, according to the newspapers, many of them *"wore mottoes in their hats calling upon their team to 'PLAY UP'"*. The weather was warm and dull, there was little wind and the ground was in *"grand condition"*. The game kicked off at seven minutes to four.

According to the 'Lancashire Daily Post': "The Higher Walton lads opened very favourably and during the first half the Reds defence was severely tried. The vigorous play of the villagers caused great enthusiasm amongst their supporters." In the second half Accrington came more into the game and missed several easy chances. The game ended in a 1-1 draw, the Higher Walton goal being scored from a "scrimmage" in front of goal. Extra time was declined by the 'Waltonians' because they had a player (Spencer) injured and were all pretty exhausted.

The 'Blackburn Times' summarised the match: "Every praise is due to Higher Walton for the plucky fight they are making for the Lancashire Cup. It was fully expected that when they met the full strength of Accrington they would disappear like chaff before the wind, but ...their play on Saturday was not one whit inferior to the 'Reds'. Had Higher Walton excelled in front of goal as they did in dash and hard work, they would have most certainly have won. Their rapid earnest play, which they kept up to the end, prevented combination among the Accrington forwards". The 'Lancashire Daily Post' said: "every man and boy must have turned out to see [the] match and when the Villagers scored the cheering was something tremendous. The little right half of Higher Walton [Tom Naylor?] repeatedly beat the international player Lofthouse. The Villagers are the pluckiest lot of fellows ever seen on the Leamington ground. In the dressing room of Higher Walton, both at starting and  at half time, there was a powerful odour of a well-advertised and celebrated oil." Does this refer to actual embrocation or a more alcoholic stimulant? This could explain the extra determination of the village team! In contrast, the Accrington supporters were "disgusted with the display of their team."

Valiant but vanquished.

The replay of the Lancashire Cup final was held at Preston North End's Deepdale ground on the following Saturday. A huge crowd of between 4000 and 6000 spectators watched the game and most of these were supporting Higher Walton. The only change in their team was a guest player, Jack Edwards, who replaced the injured Spencer. Jack was a reserve player for Preston North End and had made occasional appearances in the first team. This particular season he had played 4 games and scored 3 goals for the North End in the Football League. The Accrington team was: *Horne, Stevenson, McLennan, Haworth, Pemberton, Tattersall, Wilkinson, Bonar, Singleton, Kirkham, Lofthouse.* Joe Lofthouse had won his six England Caps whilst playing for Blackburn Rovers. The match was keenly fought and defences proved to be so good that only one goal was scored by Accrington, and that a scrappy one. Higher Walton went close at the finish but failed to score an equaliser. Chapman in goal was praised for his fine saves but the forward line of Higher Walton was criticised for its *"lack of combination"*.

Higher Walton's long cup run ended with a runners-up medal for the players but they should be given full credit for their achievements. They had beaten two teams from the Football League and lost narrowly to a third. They themselves would soon be playing in a new league – the *'Lancashire League'*.

Lancashire Football Association Cup final 1889. Runners-up silver medal awarded to Jack Mather.
(photographed with permission of the late Harry Mather)

37

Guest players.

In February 1889 Tommy Iddon of Higher Walton appeared as a guest for Preston North End Reserves in a friendly against Dundee Strathmore and played well in a 15-2 victory. The *'Lancashire Daily Post'* said *"He is a first rate player, fit on the day's form for a position in the North End's first team"*. Praise indeed.

Before the 1888-89 season ended, Higher Walton played a friendly game at Witton and their team included two special guest players: Jack Southworth and John Forbes of Blackburn Rovers. These must be the most famous players ever to turn out for the *'Villagers'*. Jack Southworth played three times for England between 1889 and 1892 and won two FA Cup winners medals. He was one of the best centre forwards of his day and his nickname was *"Skimmy"* because of his speed. In 1893 he transferred to Everton for £400. In just over one season there he scored 36 goals in 31 games, including six in one game against West Brom,

Jack Southworth

before injury forced him to retire. He was also an excellent musician and later in his life he played violin with the Hallé and other orchestras. John Forbes was a cultured and speedy full back, signed from Scotland to play in the Football League. He was a first team regular between 1889 and 1894 and won two FA Cup winners' medals. He stopped playing due to ill health but continued as a director of Blackburn Rovers. He was a successful businessman, with a gents' outfitters and sports shop on Northgate in Blackburn.

Finally, in May, Higher Walton played Preston North End's reserve team in a benefit game for their goalkeeper, Chapman. He was by all accounts a *"cool"* goalkeeper. In one game he was charged roughly by an opponent and he addressed him thus: *"Young man, just quiet yourself"*. The North End team, including famous *'Invincibles'* players Nick Ross and *'Geordie'* Drummond, were easily beaten 4-1, and this brought to an end a brilliant season for Higher Walton.

CHAMPIONS OF THE LANCASHIRE LEAGUE

William McGregor was the chairman of Aston Villa in the 1880s. He had the vision to realise that if football was to move forward as a commercial enterprise then clubs needed regular fixtures. Friendly games were often cancelled at short notice and your team could be knocked out of the FA Cup in the early rounds. McGregor was the driving force behind the first football league in the world, which played its first games in September 1888. The founder members of the Football League were six clubs from the North: Preston North End, Blackburn Rovers, Burnley, Bolton Wanderers, Everton, Accrington, and six from the Midlands: Wolverhampton Wanderers, Aston Villa, Notts County, Derby County, Stoke and West Bromwich Albion. The first league champions were Preston North End with Aston Villa the runners-up. Several clubs were unable to get into the new league, so another league, called the 'Football Alliance', was set up for the 1889-90 season. This included teams such as Darwen, Newton Heath and Bootle and it became division two of the Football League in 1892.

Baines card for Heywood Central

(photographed with permission of the National Football Museum)

The Football League was such a great success that other leagues soon appeared: the Northern League in the North East, the Birmingham & District League, the Midland League, and the Lancashire League. Higher Walton successfully applied to join the Lancashire League in its inaugural season, 1889-90. The other clubs in the league were Bury, Blackpool, Fleetwood Rangers, Heywood Central, West Manchester, Rossendale, Southport Central, Nelson, Heywood, Oswaldtwistle Rovers, Park Road (Blackburn), Hyde and Earlestown. It seems surprising that the small town of Heywood, which lies between Rochdale and Bury, should have two teams.

Top of the league.

For their first game in the new Lancashire League, Higher Walton travelled to Bury who were one of the prime movers in the formation of the league and favourites to win it. In front of 2000 spectators at Gigg Lane, Higher Walton came away with a creditable 1-1 draw. As the season progressed it was clear that there was not going to be a runaway winner, with Bury, Heywood Central, Nelson, and Blackpool all challenging for the top spot. Also in with a chance was Higher Walton. They proved to be particularly strong at home, remaining undefeated there in the league all season. Home wins included 10-0 against Earlestown, 3-2 against Heywood Central, 10-0 against Oswaldtwistle Rovers, 4-1 against Bury and 4-3 against Nelson. Only a 3-3 draw with Blackpool ruined a 100% winning record. They were less successful away from home, losing six games in total.

Earlestown were expelled from the league just a few weeks from the end of the season and this was a blow for Higher Walton. They had already beaten them twice so they lost four valuable league points. As the season drew to a close Higher Walton had to win two out of three of their last games to become champions and all three were away from home. A 2-0 victory against Park Road of Blackburn was followed by a 1-0 win at Southport. Although they lost the final game against Heywood Central 4-1 in front of 4000 spectators, the result did not matter. They had taken the championship by one point from Bury. This was a superb performance but it is unlikely that championship medals were awarded to the players, as the league was short of cash. In fact the league trophy was not purchased until the following season.

Lancashire League championship medal for 1894, awarded to 'Lol' Wright of Blackpool. This popular goalkeeper played several times against Higher Walton.
(photographed with permission of Audrey Chambers)

Lancashire League 1889-90

	pl	w	d	l	f	a	Pts
Higher Walton	**24**	**14**	**4**	**6**	**66**	**42**	**32**
Bury	24	14	3	7	65	36	31
Heywood Central	24	14	2	8	64	38	30
Nelson	24	12	4	8	55	44	28
Blackpool	24	10	6	8	61	46	26
Southport Central	24	9	7	8	40	32	25
Heywood	24	10	5	9	54	49	25
Blackburn Park Rd	24	8	6	10	44	45	22
West Manchester	24	9	4	11	44	52	22
Hyde	24	8	5	11	46	56	21
Oswaldtwistle Rvs	24	8	4	12	39	62	20
Fleetwood Rangers	24	7	5	12	35	51	19
Rossendale	24	4	3	17	37	77	11

(goals: f = for, a = against)

The Lancashire League continued until 1902-3 when it disbanded, its member clubs forming a second division of the Lancashire Combination, who then used the trophy for its competitions.

Hammered!

Not everything went well for Higher Walton in their first Lancashire League season. In October 1889 they travelled to Port Vale for a friendly game and lost 7-0 *"in miserable weather.... the players found it difficult to keep their feet"*. In the FA Cup, a bye in the first preliminary round was followed by a walkover against Park Road in the second round. Surprisingly they lost 6-2 at South Shore in the next round.

In the Lancashire Senior Cup they beat Park Road in the first round and then Halliwell in the second round. The next round was the semi-final and saw them drawn against Burnley, a powerful Football League team. The game was played on 12th April at Gigg Lane, Bury, with between two and three thousand spectators. On the day the Higher Walton team was totally outclassed and lost 7-0. The Higher Walton team was *Chapman, Daley, Rose, T.Naylor, Spencer, Baldwin, Cunliffe, Iddon, Mather, T.Naylor, E.Naylor.* Burnley's team was: *Kaye, Berry, Lang, McFetteridge, Spiers, Keenan, Hill, Stewart, Lambie, McLardie, Haresnape,* and they went on to defeat Blackburn Rovers 2-0 in the final.

LANCASHIRE LEAGUE DECLINE and FALL

For the 1890-1891 season, Park Road and Hyde were replaced by Burnley Union Star. Higher Walton managed to retain most of their better players but they were under pressure from other clubs who could afford to pay them more. They did lose two key players, Tommy Iddon and Rose, who were tempted away by Southport. In the league games up to Christmas, Higher Walton did reasonably well, winning six games and drawing two out of 15 games, but they only gained one point from the last 7 games and finished in a lowly 9th place. Bury were champions, with Blackpool runners-up. Bury would be elected to the Football League in 1894, and were FA Cup winners in 1900 and 1903, a remarkable achievement.

Manchester City & United.

Quite a few interesting friendly games were played during the season, including a game against Ardwick in Manchester. A 3-2 defeat was a good result against the team that would become *'Manchester City'* in 1894. In the FA Cup Higher Walton were drawn at home against another Manchester team, Newton Heath of the Football Alliance. They were to become *'Manchester United'* a few years later, in 1902. Higher Walton's need for cash prompted them to switch the game to Newton Heath's North Road ground. On 4th October 1890 a crowd of about 3000 spectators watched a close game that was won 2-0 by Newton Heath.

Trotters limp home.

In the Lancashire Senior Cup, Higher Walton had a tough home draw against Bolton Wanderers, who were founder members of the Football League. The *'Lancashire Daily Post'* commented *"During the present season Higher Walton has scarcely had as good a team as in the previous two seasons. The Wanderers and their supporters have looked upon the game as an easy thing, but the Waltonians made them play"* The afternoon of 7th February 1891 was fine and the ground was in good condition, with about 1000 spectators watching.

The Higher Walton team was *Chapman, Daly, E. Naylor, Baldwin, Taylor, T. Naylor, J. Mather, Mayor, W. Mather, T. Naylor, J. Blackwell.*

The Bolton team was *Sutcliffe, Somerville, Jones, Paton, Gardiner, Roberts, Barbour, Davenport, Cassidy, McNee, Monroe.* It included goalkeeper John Sutcliffe who was their regular keeper throughout the 1890s and won five caps for England. Five of the Bolton team would appear in the FA Cup final of 1894. Both teams had chances in the first half and at half time the score was 1-0 to Bolton. They scored a second goal in the second half, but the floodgates did not open and, with ten minutes to play, Baldwin scored for Higher Walton. Sadly, Higher Walton were unable to equalise but they had given the *'Trotters'* a tough game. The *'Lancashire Daily Post'* said *"The Wanderers were almost half as heavy again as their opponents and never once stood at putting their weight and size on their opponents when the Waltonians were getting dangerous. The home lads in the first half played a far too individual game. However, in the second portion they passed better and the Wanderers had all their work to keep them back at time. The first point [goal] to the Wanderers was a questionable one, Davenport being, in the opinion of nearly everyone, offside"* The newspaper commented on the Wanderers *"using their weight"* but Higher Walton obviously could give as much as they got because *"the villagers managed to send one or two of the Trotters home with rather severe scars on their legs."*

Ireland revisited.

Towards the end of the season, in March 1891, Higher Walton again travelled to Ireland to play Cliftonville of Belfast in a friendly. It is interesting to note that on the night before the game the Higher Walton team attended a *'Smoker'*. This is a *'smoking concert'* where the guests are entertained with speeches and songs. According to the *'Ulster Football'* newspaper, *"an enjoyable programme was provided and several of the Higher Walton lads favoured us with songs, which we duly appreciated."* So the players could sing as well as play football! The local press were rather critical of the game played the following day which ended in a 3-3 draw.

One reporter said, *"Whether it was from the effect of the cross-channel passage, holidaying or bad weather... Higher Walton were in anything but exhibition form. Through poaching by some of the bigger clubs over the water they have become minus some of their best men. Certainly the match was one of the rottenest I ever witnessed, neither side being able to show anything but poor play interspersed with little brilliant bits."* This was to be the last *'foreign'* trip for Higher Walton.

East Lancs Charity Shield.

As the 1890-91 season drew to a close Higher Walton did enjoy one major success in the *'East Lancs Charity Shield'* competition. Charity competitions were very common throughout the country in Victorian times. The *'East Lancs Charity Cup'* involved the bigger clubs, Blackburn Rovers, Burnley, Accrington and Darwen. Proceeds from the games went to the Blackburn & East Lancashire Infirmary. The East Lancs Charity Shield was a similar competition, but for smaller clubs. Higher Walton had already played in this competition in the previous season, losing 3-2 to Peel Bank Rovers of Church. The semi-final of 1890 saw Higher Walton drawn against fellow Lancashire Leaguers, Nelson. The game was played at Deepdale on a Saturday evening in June, in front of about 500 spectators. The Higher Walton team that night was *Chapman, Daley, Baldwin, R. Spencer, Law, Coulston, Naylor, Livesley [sic], J.Mather, Craven, W.Mather.* Nelson kicked off at 6.30pm towards the barracks (north) goal. The *'Lancashire Daily Post'* reported that, *"Higher Walton were desperately in earnest and meant to win, for before three minutes had elapsed, by dint of neat passing, they had worked the ball into their opponents half and Craven obtained the first point"* They continued to press for more goals. *"More than once Smith [the Nelson goalkeeper] had both hands full and there were two or three [players] eager to rush both goalkeeper and ball through the posts."* Jack Mather attempted this tactic and was *"seized by the neck by the goalkeeper, swung round about three times, and then 'planted' on the ground between the boards. Luckily a 'set to' between the men was averted."* Higher Walton were praised for their *"neat"* passing game whereas Nelson relied more on a *"long kicking"* game.

44

Jack Mather eventually scored a second goal, and a third was added by half time. In the second half, an exciting goalmouth scramble resulted on the ball hitting the crossbar several times before rolling between the posts for the fourth goal. Nelson got one goal back but the final score was 5-1 to Higher Walton. This was a good result considering Nelson were higher in the Lancashire League table.

Final success.

The Charity Shield Final took place on 20th June at Ewood Park, the new home of Blackburn Rovers, against Brierfield (near Nelson). The Higher Walton team was unchanged from the semi-final and the referee was Jack Forbes, the Blackburn Rovers player. The game was watched by *"barely a thousand spectators and the sun shone hotly.* The game was a somewhat one-sided affair and Higher Walton were 5-0 up by half time. The game ended in a 9-1 triumph for the Waltonians. All the players received winners' medals, and Jack Mather's was eventually passed on to his grandson, the late Harry Mather. Although Higher Walton never entered it again, the East Lancs Charity Shield competition continued  well into the twentieth century. It probably ceased after the Second World War and the final resting place of the shield is unknown.

Players depart.

Although the 1890-91 season had ended on a high note, with Higher Walton winning the Charity Shield, an ominous sign for the future was the announcement that their excellent goalkeeper Chapman was signing for the Blackburn side, Witton. Rose and Iddon were also now playing for Witton, who were trying to buy themselves a decent team to enter the Lancashire League. In contrast, Higher Walton was only a small village team that did not attract the numbers of spectators needed to pay the better players.

For the 1891-2 season Higher Walton's secretary was James Mather of 9, Victoria Terrace, the uncle of Jack and Billy Mather. The first game at home was a mid-week friendly against Blackburn Rovers, which Rovers won 5-1, with Jack Southworth scoring a hat-trick. The Higher Walton team was: *Dougle, Baldwin, Daley, Coulston, Lowe, Spencer, Taylor, Livesey, Mather, Craven, Naylor*. Another pre-season friendly in September was against Tranmere Rovers and Higher Walton travelled to the Wirral, returning with a morale-boosting 8-1 victory. The Lancashire League had gained two new teams, Witton and South Shore, but had lost Oswaldtwistle Rovers. Higher Walton could play a physical game if required and the league game away at Southport was described thus: *"Higher Walton played a rough game and soon disabled Fielding whose knee was severely injured"*.

In February they lost 3-1 at home to Blackpool and a match report said, *"one of the home backs saved his goal by kicking the ball far out into the river Darwen"*. This happened three more times during the game! In a friendly against Fishwick Ramblers, *"Whalley of Higher Walton headed into Carter's hands who saved but he was 'belgered' by Lowe"*. This refers to Jack Belger, the famous Preston North End player of the 1880s, who was famous for his charges against the unsuspecting goalkeeper, knocking keeper and ball through the posts.

Higher Walton ended their league fixtures with a similar record to the previous season, only winning 5 games and drawing 7 games, and they finished in 8th place with 17 points. However, new boys Witton had a disastrous season, conceding 111 goals and finishing next to bottom with

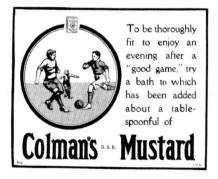

To be thoroughly fit to enjoy an evening after a "good game," try a bath to which has been added about a table-spoonful of

Colman's D.S.F. **Mustard**

only 8 points. They left the league after only one season, together with the bottom team, Heywood. The champions, for the second season running, were Bury.

Rovers again.

In the first round of the FA Cup, Higher Walton lost 5-4 to Blackpool and in the Lancashire Senior Cup they were drawn against Blackburn Rovers. Higher Walton conceded home advantage in return for a cash payment so the game was played at Ewood Park. Although the game was played in February 1892 the ground was, surprisingly, in *"excellent condition"*. The teams were Higher Walton: *Addison, Naylor, Daly, Baldwin, Law, Coulston, J.Mather, Livesey, W.Mather, Knight, Taylor.* Blackburn Rovers: *Arthur, Forrest, Forbes, Barton, Almond, Dewar, Chippendale, Campbell, Townley, Sanderson, Walton.* Blackburn Rovers showed Higher Walton some respect by playing several of their first team players. The 'Waltonians' were unable to repeat the giant killing of earlier years, but only lost 2-0. The Press summarised the game: *"Neither side exerted themselves much. The visitors' defence was good but their attack was weak".*

Founder members.

This season (1891-2) was also the first for the newly formed *'Preston & District Amateur League'* into which Higher Walton entered their reserve team. The first champions were Chorley Alliance, followed by Wheelton, Preston St Thomas, Longridge St Wilfreds, Leyland, Higher Walton Reserves, North Meols Reserves, Fulwood Rovers and Whittle-le-Woods. Therefore Higher Walton can claim to be a founder member of a local league that is still flourishing today.

New rules.

In 1892 the Lancashire League decided to standardise kick-off times but this was a major disadvantage to Higher Walton. As the *'Lancashire Daily Post'* commented: *"On Thursday a meeting was held in Bolton, at which the times for games to start during October and November were fixed. A quarter past three in October and three o'clock in November were the exact minutes pitched upon. The most inconveniently situated team in the League is Higher Walton, whose players are all working lads and cannot leave work before a quarter to one. In November they have to play at Bury and Heywood and will in consequence have to leave Preston a few minutes past eleven.*

Some of their players cannot 'get off' [work] and consequently only half a team will be able to play, their positions being filled with reserves. If 3.30pm had been fixed for November, then they could have been in nice time. Higher Walton think they have been hardly dealt with, and many followers of the game agree with them."

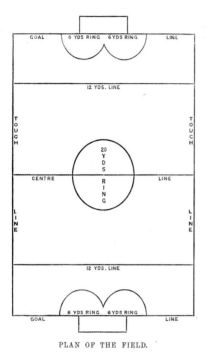

PLAN OF THE FIELD.

In 1892, as a result of changes in the laws, the Football Association introduced more pitch markings, which closely resemble those used today. The 6 yard rings were an early version of the *'6 yard box'*. Penalty kicks were introduced and a 12 yard line marked out the penalty area. The centre circle and halfway line appeared for the first time. The groundsman suddenly had a lot more work to do, marking out the pitch!

Playing Liverpool FC.

The 1892-3 season marked the departure of the last players who had been part of the great Higher Walton team in earlier years. Daly, Naylor, Baldwin and Billy Mather all signed for South Shore and W.T. Naylor for Fleetwood. The *'Preston Herald'* commented, *"It is marvellous how the villagers have kept going owing to this constant drain and it says a lot for their pluck and determination that they should come up smiling as each knockout blow is delivered"*. I doubt if anyone in Higher Walton was actually smiling at these events! The club did its best to sign replacements but they could never be as good as the players they had lost. To make matters worse the first Lancashire League game of the new season was against newly formed *'Liverpool Football Club'*, at Anfield.

Liverpool Football Club had been formed as a result of a dispute involving the owner of the Anfield ground, John Houlding, and Everton Football Club who had been playing there for eight seasons. Everton FC left and moved to nearby Goodison Park. Houlding tried to keep the name *'Everton'* but failed. He formed a new club, which he called *'Liverpool Football Club'*, in March 1892.

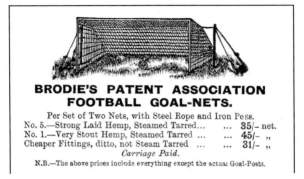

BRODIE'S PATENT ASSOCIATION FOOTBALL GOAL-NETS.

Per Set of Two Nets, with Steel Rope and Iron Pegs.

No. 5.—Strong Laid Hemp, Steamed Tarred...	...	**35/-** net.
No. 1.—Very Stout Hemp, Steamed Tarred ...	...	**45/-** „
Cheaper Fittings, ditto, not Steam Tarred ...	...	**31/-** „

Carriage Paid.

N.B.—The above prices include everything except the actual Goal-Posts.

Goal nets were introduced in 1892. They were not compulsory but soon became popular. They were made from hemp rope, which is made from the marijuana plant! They were patented in 1891 by John Alexander Brodie, who in later years became the Chief Engineer of the City of Liverpool and the Mersey tunnel.

Liverpool signed some good players, the majority of them Scots, but failed to get his team into division two of the Football League. He was forced to enter the team into the smaller Lancashire League. Their very first league fixture was at Anfield, on 3rd September 1892, against a struggling Higher Walton team.

The *'Villagers'* arrived 45 minutes late, with only 10 men, and were predictably hammered 8-0. Only a small crowd of between 200 and 300 watched the game due to the fact that most fans were still loyal to Everton. However, gates at Anfield soon increased to between 1000 and 4000 for the rest of the season. Liverpool finished the season as champions, but only on goal average, as Blackpool had an identical points total. The following season they were champions of division two of the Football League and moved on to future glories in division one, the Premiership and Europe. Higher Walton were moving in the opposite direction!

Higher Walton predictably lost the return game against Liverpool on 22nd October 1892, but only 5-0. Perhaps the poor state of the pitch helped their cause. The 150 supporters who watched the game was probably the smallest crowd ever to witness a Liverpool league game. An account of the game in the *'Bootle Times'* stated *"Liverpool are still going in good style, and on Saturday they defeated Higher Walton by five goals to nil. The ground they had to play on was in a very bad state, the players being up to their ankles in mud. There would be only about 150 spectators present when the game was commenced, Liverpool doing pretty much as they liked with the home team, Miller scoring two goals before half time. After the kick-off Wylie defeated the home custodian once and Miller twice and won a tame game."* The Higher Walton team of three years earlier would certainly have given Liverpool a closer game.

Hard times.

Higher Walton struggled throughout the season and were outclassed in most Lancashire League games. With the team not doing well, local support had dwindled and only a handful of spectators watched home games. This was in contrast to the crowds of hundreds and sometimes thousands who watched away games. Higher Walton was now a village team struggling to play in a semi-professional league. On 1st October they managed to gain a 3-3 draw against South Shore. The Higher Walton team was unrecognisable from that of earlier years and was *Addison, Enderby, Moon, Gerrard, Lowe, Flintoff, Forest, Parker, Knight, Livesley [sic], Booth*. In fact the South Shore team was more familiar and contained several ex-Walton players: *Naylor, Daley, Baldwin and Billy Mather*.

In the FA Cup they did manage to get through the first qualifying round, beating Ashton Town 3-2 in Manchester but in the next round they lost 5-1 at home to Fleetwood Rangers. The local Fleetwood paper had a colourful account of the trip to Higher Walton. It included the trip from Preston railway station by horse drawn wagonette across the River Ribble, some sarcastic comments about the small size of the crowd and the fact that goalkeeper Chapman was now playing for Fleetwood. Read it for yourself:

THE RANGERS ROMP ROUND HIGHER WALTON.

It was a merry and enthusiastic party that accompanied the Rangers to a 'rural Preston' on Saturday, as it was generally looked upon as being an easy thing. On Preston being reached I joined at a 'cart' with the rest of 'em, and we left the noise and bustle of the "proud town" behind us. The scenery was fascinating, being a landscape of well-wooded hills relieved at the foot by the crystal surface of the 'Ribble'. When we arrived at the ground we thought we were a "hundred fathoms" too soon, as only about half a dozen enthusiastic Waltonians occupied one corner of the field. The clerk of the weather appeared to be in a bad temper, for it rained incessantly. The ground was more like a 'herring pond' than anything else and the players had to 'paddle their own canoes'. About 6,000 spectators - oh, less than that – sixty, lined the enclosure and each team on wading into the field met with a cordial reception, Craven, especially being 'greeted' by the home supporters.

Footballers Note!

FOR
COUGHS.

TRADE MARK
REGISTERED

Owbridge's
Lung Tonic

FOR
COLDS.

Football spectators run greater
risks than players.

DAMP GROUND—COLD WINDS.

At the first sign of cold or chill take
OWBRIDGE'S.

Beware of Substitutes.

The Waltonians elected to play with the strong wind at their backs but the Rangers at once bombarded the home citadel, and Robinson scored three minutes from the start. The Rangers pressed, but threw away chance after chance. "Can't ta bundle it an't chap between sticks through?" roared a Fleetwooder from the 'stand' - beg pardon, but he was 'on the stand' all the same. See? Addison fisted out, and Livesey ran the ball down. In his attempt to clear Colley missed his kick, and Forrest getting hold equalised amid a peal of thunder from the 'thimble-full' of home supporters. Forrest was cheered, even by the Fleetwood contingent for his dashing runs, but he was too selfish on many occasions. A minute later Craven, who was continually hooted by the Waltonians, compelled Addison to throw out. Brogan put in some fine work and scored a second for the Rangers [who] played a superior game all round.

'Oliver', who was a spectator, in the disguise of a soldier, stopped the ball.... Half-time arrived with the score 2-0 in favour of the visitors. A splendid cross by Robinson was then turned to account by Brogan. The homesters now made a determined attempt at combination and for the first time got in the vicinity of the visitors' goal, but Chapman saved well. Brogan made a splendid run and ended up by scoring a fourth. Walton retaliated vigorously, and scored from a free kick, but the point was disallowed. Herbert Wilson, who had been playing a champion game got hurt and was of no further use. The Rangers, however, put on a fifth point, and the whistle sounded time with the score 5-1. "It's rained and poured deawn," as a villager said, when we got into the open wagonette But the irrepressible 'Oliver' was there, and sang us several songs, before saying, in a faltering tone, farewell to his 'friends of yore'.

The *'Preston Herald'* gave a somewhat different account of the same game. They reported that one Higher Walton player failed to turn up and the village team started the game with only 10 men. Fleetwood scored soon after the kick-off but were fortunate because *"one of the home backs thinking Brogan, who wore a jersey similar to Higher Walton, was one of his own players. Colley, the Fleetwood back, was similarly attired"*. Although this colour clash was pointed out to the referee, he did nothing about it, and it caused further problems and ill feeling throughout the game. By the end of the season Higher Walton had only won 3 out of 22 league games and were rock bottom of the league.

FINAL CURTAIN (1893-5)

For the 1893-94 season Higher Walton sensibly resigned from the Lancashire League and entered the local *'Preston and District Amateur League'*. Although they were now a small village team, they still entered the FA Cup competition. In the first preliminary round they were drawn away to Workington but they did not fulfil the fixture, and *'scratched'*. This was probably because of the high cost of travelling to Cumberland with little hope of winning.

Higher Walton also entered in the Lancashire Senior Cup and were beaten 11-0 by Rossendale at Rawtenstall. The Senior Cup was really intended for the top 20 teams in Lancashire and it was surprising that Higher Walton was put in this category. Perhaps it was the influence of Richard Iddon who was still on the Committee of the Lancashire FA.

Strangely, they were also entered in the Lancashire Amateur Cup, because they now qualified as an amateur team. Normally a team could only enter one of these cup competitions. They played away at Westhoughton Albion in February 1894 and lost 2-1. The game was the subject of an appeal to the Lancashire FA. Higher Walton claimed that their opponents had played a professional called Holt. The Lancashire FA rejected the appeal and the result stood. Higher Walton were censured for *"leaving the field early"*. In the Preston and District league they played 16 games and managed to hold their own, finishing in mid table, with Preston Athletic the champions.

Preston & District League 1893-94

	pl	w	d	l	Pts
Preston Athletic	13	9	2	2	20
Leyland	14	8	3	3	19
Wheelton	12	8	2	2	18
Chorley Alliance	14	7	4	4	17
Higher Walton	**15**	**5**	**5**	**5**	**15**
Whittle-le-Woods	14	5	6	6	13
Walton-le-Dale	12	5	7	7	10
Chorley St Georges	16	1	11	11	6
Heapey Institute	12	1	10	10	3

Final farewell.

The following season, 1894-95, Higher Walton did not even enter the Preston & District League and this was another indication of their decline. The team played very few games and was on the verge of extinction. With little preparation or practice they travelled to Oswaldtwistle in January 1895 to play in the Lancashire Junior Cup. They inevitably lost the game 9-1 with Moon scoring their only goal. This was probably the final game of the first, and greatest, Higher Walton team. However, there were other teams playing in the village and one of these, Higher Walton Albion, became the main team for the next two decades.

HIGHER WALTON ALBION (1894-1914)

In the 1894-95 season a team called *'Higher Walton Albion'* started to play friendly games against local teams in the Preston area. In January 1895 the Albion beat St Paul's Reserves 5-3, the Higher Walton team being *T.Davies, Jack Burton, J.Walton, J.Mather, T.Walker, J.Davies, Charles Clarke, R.Morton, J.Livesey, J.Baron, R.Turner*. Some players had probably played for the first Higher Walton team: for example, Jack Mather and Jimmy Livesey. The following season, friendly games were arranged against teams which included Dutch Barn Rovers (lost 3-4), Fulwood Athletic (won 5-0) and Higher Walton Excelsiors (won 3-0). The *'Preston Herald'* recorded that the first game was played *"at Hoghton Lane"* so we cannot assume the team always played in the centre of the village.

HIGHER WALTON ALBION (mid 1890s)
The only players definitely identified are Charles Clarke (far left) and Jack Burton (far right) who were brothers-in-law. The team is probably arranged as they played on the pitch. The goalkeeper is in the centre of the back row with two full backs on either side. The three half-backs are seated and the five forwards are at the front. Matt Livesey is probably second from the left on the front row. The centre-forward may be one of the 'old Invincible Waltonians', possibly Tommy Iddon. At least two players are wearing shin pads on the outside of the socks, in 1880s style

Amateur hour.

The 1896-97 season was a landmark for the Albion team as they entered a new league: the *"Preston Amateur League"*. New leagues appeared and disappeared throughout the 1890s and this one was destined to be short lived. The *'Preston Herald'* reported that, *"The advent of the new Amateur League has been hailed with enthusiasm."* The maximum number of clubs in the league was to be twelve and nine entered for this first season. These were Cannon Street, Ashton, Catterall, Longridge, Moor Park, Preston Alliance, Preston Catholic Grammar School and St Paul's. Clubs had to be based within a 12 mile radius of Preston Town Hall and because of a shortage of referees, each club had to nominate one person to officiate in other games. The winners of the championship would get silver medals.

Higher Walton Albion's first game was against a *"new organisation"*, Cannon Street. The visitors arrived 20 minutes late and the game kicked off at 3.40pm. The Higher Walton team was *Woods, Lowe, Jack Burton, Doran, Jones, James Kay, Charles Clarke, Matt Livesey, WH (Billy) Mather, Joseph Kay and Walker*. The *'Preston Herald'* reported that *"It was evident from the commencement that the pace was to be a scorcher"*. Billy Mather scored the first goal and by half time Albion were 2-0 ahead. However, the strong wind was now in favour of the visitors and they attacked repeatedly. After 20 minutes, *"J. Langton secured the ball and after beating no less than four opponents, scored a really magnificent goal for the visitors"*. Soon after this, Higher Walton conceded an own goal. The home supporters realised that defeat was on the cards and *"two or three hundred supporters made themselves heard as if they were thousands"*. All this proved in vain as Cannon Street scored the winning goal five minutes from time.

Cannon Street and Higher Walton were to prove to be the two best teams in the league and by Christmas both were top of the league with 11 points. Higher Walton had a far superior goal average, having scored 31 goals in 7 games, including wins of 7-0 against Catterall, 8-1 against Longridge and 5-1 against Preston Alliance. Top goalscorers were Matt Livesey, Jack Burton and Charles Clarke.

The return game against Cannon Street was played at 'The Pleasure Gardens' on 25th November 1896 and predictably ended in a 2-2 draw, with Higher Walton equalising in the last four minutes. The team was *Woods, brothers Lowe, Rodgetts, Jones, S.Livesey, C.Clarke, M.Livesey, Iddon, Kay, J.Burton* (this is possibly the lineup shown in the team photograph on page 54).

Brookhouse Rules.

Unfortunately we do not know what happened in the second half of the season and who ended up champions, because no newspaper reports are available. We could hazard a guess that Higher Walton

Gold medal awarded to Charles Clarke

were runners up to Cannon Street. A runners-up medal, belonging to Charles Clarke, does exist for this season but for a different competition, the 'Brookhouse'. In later years, a competition with this name took place on a private ground off Eldon Street in Preston. It gained notoriety in the 1920s because the laws of the game were often overlooked and it was not unusual to see fights during and after the games. These were referred to as *"The Brookhouse Rules"*. This medal may be evidence that this competition took place in the 1890s, or it may be another with the same name.

Preston and District.

For the 1897-98 season, Higher Walton Albion entered the Preston & District League. Their opponents were School Lane, Chorley Alliance, Farington Mill, Banks, Southport Reserves, Brownedge, Whittle-le-Woods, Kirkham and Leyland Reserves. In October 1897 Albion played local rivals School Lane, and won 5-0, with goals scored by Burton, Almond and Livesey. The secretary at that time was Mr T. Parker of Taberner Terrace on Hoghton Lane.

In January 1899 they played a home game against Chorley Reserves. The *'Preston Herald'* reported, *"Chorley Reserve, who are at present champions of the Preston & District League, were the visitors at Higher Walton on Saturday. The home team turned out in new colours of the 'old invincible Higher Walton', chocolate and blue, and presented a very smart appearance."* The home team started badly and Chorley were unlucky not to score. However, Higher Walton began to *"infuse more life into their play"* and were awarded a penalty after 25 minutes for hand ball. Livesey, the captain of Higher Walton, scored from the spot. In the second half *"Morton slipped in and nipped the bud of Chorley for the second time, amid loud cheers. The visitors now played like a beaten team and the game ended 2-0 to Higher Walton"*

Higher Walton Albion stayed in the Preston & District League until the 1900-01 season, then, after a short break, they returned to the League in 1907.

HIGHER WALTON ALBION, early 1900s. The possible order of players is back row, left to right : Cornelius Moon, Pat Delaney, Jonathan Hargreaves, Matt Smith, J.Sharples, G.Clarke, G.Morris, J.Morton, W.Sharples, W.Patterson.
Front row: J.Cook, S.Walsh, Lewis Naylor, James Coleman Clarke, John R Delaney
(photograph reproduced with permission of Norman Hayes)

Their record for the 1907-8 season was: played 26, won 13, drew 5, lost 8, goals for 78, goals against 62, points 31, position 6th out of 14. In the following season (1908-9) they reached the semi-final of the Guildhall Cup competition. This cup was, and still is, the main cup competition for teams in the Preston & District League. The cup was presented by the owners of the Grand Clothing Hall on Guildhall Street, Preston in 1905, and was originally known as the *'Grand Clothing Hall Cup Competition'*. The photograph of the Higher Walton Albion team on page 57 may have been taken around this time.

In 1909-10 Higher Walton Albion were still in division 1 of the Preston & District League, and they also had a reserve team, in division 2. The league record was excellent (played 16, won 11, drawn 3, lost 2, goals for 54, goals against 25, points 25) and they ended the season as runners up to Leyland Red Rose. Other teams in division 1 included Clayton Green, School Lane Athletic, Walton-le-Dale, Penwortham, Frenchwood, St Joseph's and Christ Church. In the 1910-11 season they played 19 games (won 9, drew 3 and lost 7, goals for 54, goals against 38, points 21) and finished in 5th place, with the reserve team being runners-up in division 2.

Champions again.

For the 1911-12 season Higher Walton Albion entered the West Lancashire League, a league which had originally been formed in 1905 as the *'Preston & District Combination'*. They made an excellent start to the season, winning the first seven games on the trot. They continued this form throughout the season, only losing 5 games, and finished seven points ahead of their nearest rivals, Leyland.

WEST LANCASHIRE LEAGUE 1911 -12

	pl	w	d	l	f	a	Pts
Higher Walton	**26**	**20**	**1**	**5**	**79**	**37**	**41**
Leyland	26	15	4	7	56	32	34
Adlington	26	16	2	8	64	44	34
Fleetwood	26	15	3	8	67	38	33
Horwich RMI	26	13	6	7	64	41	32
Coppull Central	26	9	7	10	42	40	25
Hamilton Central	26	9	6	11	50	58	24
Walton-le-Dale	26	8	7	11	51	64	23
Brinscall Rovers	26	7	8	11	40	59	22
Longridge	26	7	7	12	39	45	21
Lytham Athletic	26	9	3	14	51	64	21
Chorley Reserve	26	8	4	14	50	58	20
Kirkham	26	8	2	16	34	69	18
Morecambe	26	5	6	15	36	64	16

On 1st April 1912, Higher Walton clinched the championship by beating Fleetwood 4-1. According to the *'Lancashire Daily Post'*: *"Both teams were strongly represented, and a keenly contested game was witnessed. For the homesters, Brindle, Halsall, Naylor and Delaney were prominent players"*.

HIGHER WALTON. Champions, West Lancashire League 1911-12.
Back row, left to right: J.Thornley, J.Crook, W.Brewer, J.Dagger, D.Brogan, T.Horrocks, Cornelius Moon (Treasurer). Middle row: G.Crook (Trainer), W.Thornley, J. Morton, J.Thistleton, W.Brindle, Pat Delaney, J.Coupe, R.Freeman, W.Gore, J.Sharples (Secretary). Front row: G.Thornley, W.Knowles (captain), Lewis Naylor, W.Dawson, W.France, H.Halsall, E.Kerin (Chairman)
(source: Lancs Daily Post handbook)

The following season (1912-13) Chorley Reserves and Morecambe left the league and were replaced by Southport Central reserves, Freckleton & Chorley St Peter's. The *'Lancashire Daily Post'* said that *"Higher Walton have paid the penalty of fame by losing many good men, but generally they can field efficient substitutes"*. In fact they still had many of the players from the championship season and by Christmas were near the top of the table. However, following a defeat in the Richardson Cup and a series of poor results in February 1913, the club disappeared from the league.

The reason for the demise of the team is unclear but whatever the reason, all football was soon to be seriously disrupted by the First World War and some players would never return from the conflict.

Pat Delaney was one of the best players in the village at this time. He was good enough to have trials with a professional club, Queens Park Rangers of the Southern league. During the First World War he played for an Army team against an Irish team. He survived the war and returned to Higher Walton, but he suffered some after-effects of a gas attack. Then aged 31, his best football years were behind him. He lived above the butcher's shop at 12, Cann Bridge Street.

Pat Delaney

War hero.

James Coleman Clarke

(photograph reproduced with permission of George Rounding)

James Coleman Clarke played for Higher Walton Albion before 1912 and was the younger brother of Charles Clarke, who had played in the mid-1890s. James decided to start a new life by emigrating to Australia in 1912. During the First World War he volunteered to join the Australian army in December 1915. He served in the 45th Battalion of the Australian infantry and he probably dreamed that while he was fighting in France he might have a chance to visit his home village in England. This was not to be. He was wounded in action and tragically died of his wounds at a hospital in Boulogne on 12th August 1916.

James Coleman Clark was one of the fifty four villagers who never returned from the war and who are commemorated on the war memorial in All Saints churchyard.

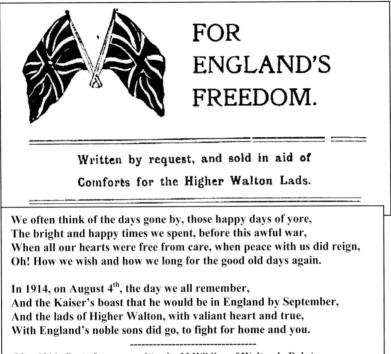

FOR ENGLAND'S FREEDOM.

Written by request, and sold in aid of

Comforts for the Higher Walton Lads.

We often think of the days gone by, those happy days of yore,
The bright and happy times we spent, before this awful war,
When all our hearts were free from care, when peace with us did reign,
Oh! How we wish and how we long for the good old days again.

In 1914, on August 4th, the day we all remember,
And the Kaiser's boast that he would be in England by September,
And the lads of Higher Walton, with valiant heart and true,
With England's noble sons did go, to fight for home and you.

(May 1916. Part of a poem written by M.Wilding of Walton-le-Dale.)

BETWEEN THE WARS (1920-1940)

League football resumed after the war and Higher Walton re-appeared in the Preston & District League in the 1920-21 season. This team was probably a continuation of the pre-war team, but it was now, for one season, called *'Higher Walton United'*. Other teams in the league were Penwortham, L&NW Loco, Garstang, Walmer Bridge, Walton-le-Dale, Leyland Motors, Fylde Billiard Hall. Eccleston Parish, Brookhouse Rangers, Gregson Lane, Dick Kerrs Reserves, Farington Villa and Alexandra Rovers.

Albert the great.

Around this time, a goalkeeper called Albert McInroy played a few games for Higher Walton. He was born in Walton-le-Dale in 1901 and as a schoolboy he played on the wing. He worked at Preston Co-op and Leyland Rubber as a packer and played games for several local teams, including Higher Walton. He signed as an amateur for Preston North End in 1921. Although he was with North End for two seasons he only played two reserve games and was released in February 1923. He joined Leyland Motors as a professional in November 1922 and in May 1923 he signed for Sunderland. Years later Albert recalled that he was signed, *"in the lavatory of the Grand Hotel in Manchester, down below, two minutes after midnight. My contract with Leyland expired at midnight.... Bob Kyle [the*

manager] sent Leyland two fifties. I got ten pounds: two five pound notes in my pocket. I was a millionaire". He went on to play a total of 496 first class games for Sunderland, Newcastle, Leeds and Gatehead. Some comments made at the time about his play include, *"He is one of the smartest and most daring goalkeepers in England"; "He sets himself in such a manner that he is never bowled over by charging opponents"*; and he is, *"a bundle of agility"*. Albert won one England cap (against Ireland) and a cup winner's medal for Newcastle United in 1932. He was remembered by the late Harry Brewer, aged 95 in 2004, who had himself played for Higher Walton in the late 1920s.

Schoolboy football in the 1920s.

Harry Brewer attended Higher Walton (All Saints) school in the early 1920s. Schoolboy football was the starting point for future adult footballers. Most pupils left school at the age of fourteen, so school teams consisted of boys aged thirteen or younger.

It was in the 1920s that the Higher Walton school team became a force in local football competitions. Many of these were sponsored by local businesses, who supplied the cup and medals for the winners. In those days, these were usually good quality gold or silver medals. After the First World War, Frederick Dugdale Jones was the Headmaster of Higher Walton (All Saints) Church School. He took over from Kathleen Ferrier's father, William, in 1914 and remained there until his retirement in 1944. He was particularly interested in natural history and sport, encouraging the girls to play rounders and the boys football. The football team was allowed to train on Eastham's field opposite the school, across the brook.

The boys' football team was the first winner of the *'VH Gatty Challenge Cup'* in June 1921 and each player received a gold and silver medal. The donor of this Cup was F.Gatty & Co., an important local employer. Their Bannister Hall dye works was situated about half a mile up the River Darwen. Gattys made their fortune from a patent dyeing process for khaki cloth, which was supplied to the armed forces in two world wars. They opened their works in Higher Walton in 1894 and it finally closed in 1964. In the following season, in May 1922, the school team won the *'Dewhurst Cup'*, a competition dating back to 1912. In the final they beat St Leonard's of Walton-le-Dale (2-1) and this was the first time they had won the cup.

In 1925 the team won four different trophies in one year! In June they won the *'St Saviour's Recreation Club Schoolboy Challenge Cup'* and, according to the school logbook, *"twelve very handsome gold medals were presented to the team".* In July they won the *'Dewhurst Cup'* for a second time, beating St Aidan's of Bamber Bridge 3-2 in the final.

Medals won by James B Clarke in 1925: the *'St Saviours Cup'* (right) and the *'Dewhurst Cup'* (left) (medals now in the possession of George Rounding)

As a reward, the team was taken on a trip to the Lake District in a charabanc and they visited Windermere, Rydal and Grasmere. The Headmaster, Mr Jones, commented: *"It was a real education for the boys – the district was quite new and wonderful to them"*.

The successful All Saints school team, 1924-5. Back row, left to right: John Smith, Mr Burgess (vicar), Norman Whittle, Frank Greenaway, Robert Mansley, Billy Rylance, George King, Ronald Mansley, Mr Greenaway, Mr Jones (headmaster), Front row: Harry Brewer, James Burton Clarke, Sidney Scholes, Tommy Anderton, Jack Bamford, Stanley Daggers. (Photograph loaned by Miss Anne Bradley)

In September the team won another cup, the *'Leyland Tradesman's Cup'*, beating St Andrew's of Leyland 5-3 in the final. To celebrate, a treat was arranged for the whole school in the form of a potato pie supper and concert. Finally, in December, they beat Lostock Hall 2-0 in the final of the *'Daily Dispatch Cup'*.

The school team would never again match the achievements of 1925 but won the *'St Saviours Cup'* again in June 1926, beating Bamber Bridge Wesleyans 3-1 in the final. Some of these schoolboy players would play for the village team in future years. Jim Clarke went on to play for Farington Villa but his elder brother Harold became captain of Higher Walton in the 1930s.

Playing in the YMCA.

In the 1920-21 season, in addition to the first team which played in the Preston & District League, Higher Walton had a reserve team which played in the smaller Preston YMCA League. This league grew in importance through the 1920s and even brought about the temporary demise of the Preston & District League in 1928. Higher Walton disappeared from the Preston & District League in 1921 but by the 1926-27 season they were back in division 3 of the YMCA League.

By the 1929-30 season they had risen to division 1 of the YMCA league, finishing 9th out of 14 teams. Other teams were Farington Villa, Moor Park, Whittle-le-Woods, Goosnargh United, Loyal Regiment, Bretherton, Leyland Motors, Lostock Hall, Gas Company, West End, Leyland Paints, Horrockses and Thomas Drydens. In April 1930 Higher Walton reached the final of the YMCA Cup for the first time, by beating Horrockes 7-5 in a replayed semi-final. The final against Longridge was played at Preston North End's Deepdale ground on the evening of 29th April with a kick-off time of 7.15pm.

YMCA Cup 1929-30, winners gold medal awarded to Harold Clarke

Higher Walton won the final in front of 2,060 spectators. A photograph of the victorious team appeared in the 'Lancashire Daily Post', although final score was not recorded. It shows J.Pearson, S.Scholes, R.Dickinson, William Woods (mascot), Harold Clark (capt), J.Strangway, J.Balshaw, Lew Naylor (trainer), W.Sharples, B.Sharples, W.Moulding, R.Saul, T.Briggs, T.Sharples and Hubert Woods (secretary).

In the 1930-31 season they finished 3rd out of 14 teams in Division 1 of the YMCA League. The 1930s was to prove to be a very successful decade for Higher Walton in cup competitions as they reached a total of six finals and won two of them.

HIGHER WALTON FC, late 1920s or early 1930s.
Standing, left to right, Hubert Woods (secretary), Jack Sharples *("Jack Fish")*,
three unknown, then R.Saul, T.Briggs and two unknown. Front row, Bob Sharples,
Harold Clarke, - Delaney and Walter Sharples, then two unknown.
(Photograph reproduced with permission of Marlene Short)

It is commonly thought that the Preston & District League
disbanded in 1928 for eight years but this is not quite true, because
the league reappeared for one season in 1931-32. Higher Walton
entered this league and had a very successful season. They had a
superb record (played 26, won 24, drawn 1 lost 1, goals for 164,
goals against 49, points 49) but Goosnargh United went one better.
They lost no games all season and finished with 51 points. Higher
Walton also reached the final of the *'Guildhall Cup'*, beating
Grimsargh United 3-1 in the semi-final. The players in that game
were *Winter, Costigan, Robinson, Murphy, H. Clarke, Baron, Walpole,
Moulding, Kirby, Bentham and Sharples.* The Secretary was Mr
Sharples and trainer Mr Higham. A photograph of this team
appeared in the *'Lancashire Daily Post'* of 1st March 1932. The final
was held at Deepdale on Thursday 21st April 1932 with a kickoff
time of 6.45pm, in fine weather and in front of 1,433 spectators.
Higher Walton lost 3-1 to their league rivals Goosnargh, with
Harold Clarke scoring the consolation goal.

Balancing the books.

For the 1932-33 season Higher Walton were back in division 1 of the YMCA league and they finished fourth, with Whittle & Clayton-le-Woods the champions. They also reached the final of the YMCA cup, beating Longridge 2-1 in the semi-final, but they lost to Ribbleton Avenue Wesleyans in the final. The final was held at Deepdale on 26th April 1933, with a 6.45pm kick off, and 1,090 watched the game. In the following season (1933-34) they were runners-up in the league, with Longridge United the champions.

Hubert Woods was the Secretary through the 1930s and his granddaughter, Marlene Short, still has the account book for the 1934-35 season. Total income for the season was £38, from a jumble sale (£4.50), donations from various individuals and several raffles. The weekly raffle prizes included cigarettes, a hen, rabbits or mutton! Spectators had to pay to watch the games and total gate receipts of about £8 came from 10 league and 2 cup games, with the local derby against Walton-le-Dale contributing the most. Expenses included, *"YMCA entrance fee and fixture books, 2 pounds"* (£2), *"Lancashire FA fee, 3 shillings"* (15p), *"Field rent, 10 pounds"* (£10), *"iodine & ointment, one shillings"* (5p), *"Bladder & laces, 2 shillings"* (10p), *"washing, 5 shillings"* (25p). *"cigarettes, 5 shillings"* (25p, presumably for the raffle and not the players!). Referees expenses including *"coffee"* were seven shillings (35p) per game, which would be worth about £16 in 2006. The club also purchased a wreath for the funeral of Mr J. Sharples who had been the secretary in earlier years.

Second best.

In the 1935-36 season, Higher Walton were again challenging for honours. They were runners-up to Waverley FC in the league and got through to the final of the YMCA challenge cup. This was held at Dick, Kerr's ground at Ashton Park on the evening of Tuesday 28th April 1936 and their opponents were Leyland Motors. Heavy rain during the first half resulted in scrappy play and defences dominated the game.

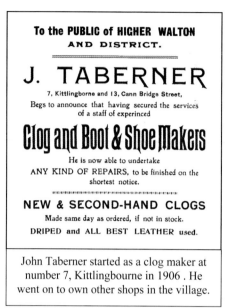
John Taberner started as a clog maker at number 7, Kittlingbourne in 1906 . He went on to own other shops in the village.

The game was fully reported in the *'Lancashire Daily Post'*. *'Wayfarer'* noted *"Both sides were excitable and in one fierce attack by Higher Walton the Motors keeper, Aldred, received a kick on the head when he flung himself on the ball. He was temporarily knocked out and while he was being attended to several spectators ran onto the pitch and there was a general scramble. Order was eventually restored but Aldred had to leave the pitch, his place being taken in goal by the Motors centre forward. Within a few minutes he was beaten when he let a shot from Robinson bounce through his arms."* The Motors equalised soon after. *"The standard of play like the weather improved after the interval, Higher Walton playing much better. Bates, the Higher Walton goalkeeper, made two fine saves then his side went ahead through Patterson."* However, the Motors scored twice more and their defence held out to the final whistle, resulting in a 3-2 victory. According to *'Wayfarer*, Motors were lucky to win. *"Walmsley the Higher Walton captain and centre half was the best man on the field, his constructive and defensive work being nearly flawless. Sharples played well on the right, and Milsom and Sumner, the backs, were reliable....the forwards were not as good as those of the Motors"*.

Two on the trot.

The following season they again reached the final of the YMCA Cup, defeating Ribbleton 10-3, Penwortham Amateurs 12-0, Croston Rangers 7-0 and Farington Celtic 1-0 along the way. The cup final was this time played at Deepdale on Saturday 6th March 1937, kick off 3.15pm. The weather was fine and a massive crowd of 5,443 watched the game. The opponents were again Leyland Motors.

Higher Walton were favourites, having been unbeaten in the league, but they failed to live up to expectations and lost 4-2. One of the key players that season was the captain J.Walmsley, but he did not play in the final. The Higher Walton team that day was: *F.Bates, F.Milsom, Dick Sumner, Knight, Sharples, Jimmy Pearson, Charlie Winter, L.Slingsby, F.Heys, Robinson and George Patterson.*

'Wayfarer' in the *'Lancashire Post'* wrote: *"one thing cannot be disputed and that is the better side won. It was a great victory for Leyland Motors for not only did they inflict on Higher Walton their first defeat of the season but established a precedent by winning the trophy for two consecutive seasons. In view of Higher Walton's wonderful record this season….I was disappointed with their display. True, they equalised twice after being a goal down-they certainly did not lack courage-but the forwards were definitely below form, particularly Robinson and Patterson who missed several good chances. Strangely enough they scored Higher Walton's two goals. For the defence I have nothing but praise. The halfbacks, with Sharples outstanding, strove manfully until the end and Milsom gave one of the best exhibitions of full back play I have seen for a long time. Bates, in goal was beaten 4 times but gave a brilliant display…..repeatedly diving at the threatening feet of the Chorley forwards. Higher Walton spoiled their chances with over eagerness, the players often getting in each other's way. Knight was carried off injured through a collision with Milsom. I saw one forward dispossess another as much as to say 'Here I'll show you how it should be done'. Walton often flung all their resources into attack and found themselves represented by only Bates, Milsom and Sumner in their own half… I think both teams may be congratulated on a sporting display."*

Third time lucky.
The team was still good enough to reach a third consecutive Cup final in 1938 and this time they triumphed, beating Penwortham on Easter Monday, 18th April, at Leyland Motors ground. The team that day was *F.Bates (goal), F.Milsom, Dick Sumner (full backs), W.Curtis, Bill Whittle, Jimmy Pearson (half backs), Charlie Winter, L.Slingsby, F.Heys, J.Milsom and George Patterson (forwards).* Their trainer was Fred *('Nick')* Livesey.

A photograph of the victorious team appeared in the *'Lancashire Daily Post'* on Wednesday 18th April 1938. Hubert Wood's granddaughter, Marlene Short, has a photograph of this team with the YMCA Cup and has allowed us to reproduce it below.

HIGHER WALTON 1937-38, YMCA CUP WINNERS.
Standing, left to right: Fred (*'Nick'*) Livesey (trainer), J.Watson, Ray Hardacre, Jack Sharples (*'Jack Fish'*), F.Milsom, F.Bates, Dick Sumner, Chris Lerning, Billy Livesey. Seated: W.Curtis, Bill Whittle, Jimmy Pearson, Hubert Woods. Kneeling: Charlie Winter, L.Slingsby, F.Heys, J.Milsom, George Patterson.

During the 1920s and 1930s Jack Sharples, a local character who had the nickname *'Jack Fish'*, appears as a supporter on many team photographs. Higher Walton played in the YMCA league throughout the 1930s, always in division 1. During the 1939-40 season a dispute arose between the YMCA League and the Preston Referees Society over a proposed reduction of fees from 5 shillings to 3 shillings and sixpence. After several weeks impasse the league backed down and fixtures were completed. Higher Walton finished 4th out of 8 teams but the outbreak of the Second World War was to seriously disrupt normal football. Many teams gave up for the duration of the war and, in Higher Walton's case, it was for even longer.

HIGHER WALTON UNITED (1953-2005)

In 1946, after the Second World War ended, the only team playing in the village was *'Higher Walton Mills'* who played in the YMCA league. However, in 1953 a match was arranged on King George V playing fields between married and single men, as part of the Coronation celebrations. After the game, some of the players decided to form a new team, to be called *'Higher Walton United'*, with Jimmy Crook as secretary. They joined the YMCA league for the 1953-54 season and did well, finishing just behind champions Higher Walton Mills. They entered the Preston & District league in the 1954-55 season and Tom Counsell took over as secretary. In addition they ran a reserve team in the YMCA league. According to Preston & District League handbooks of the time, the team first played in green shirts with white collars (up to 1957-8) but, from the 1960s, red became the established colour of strip, through to the 2005 season. At this time the team was changing on the King George V playing fields in a wooden pavilion that was just to the right of the pitch, where the bowling green and community centre stand today. On the left hand side of the park was a grass area that had been used for allotments during the war.

Fame in the fifties.

The team soon became a force in the Preston & District League and were champions of the *'B'* division in the 1954-55 season. Gregson Lane had a team in the *'B'* division during the 1950s and their secretary at that time, Frank Thompson, recalls the league game played at Higher Walton one evening. This local derby attracted a large crowd, with opposing supporters facing each other across the pitch. Gregson Lane knew that they would find it difficult to beat Higher Walton so they brought in an illegal player, a *'ringer'*, who normally played in the Lancashire Combination for Fleetwood. Passions were high, with players and spectators getting over-excited, but the game ended in an honourable draw. Soon after, Higher Walton signed Gregson Lane's best player, Derek Randall.

Higher Walton were champions of the 'A' division in the following season, 1955-56, and their record was, played 24, won 17, drew 4, lost 3, goals for 86, goals against 35. They had a strong team throughout the 1950s and were 'A' Division Champions again in 1958-59. Finally, in the 1959-60 season, they won the Guildhall Cup for the first and only time, beating English Electric 2-0 in the final at Deepdale in front of 2,194 spectators.

English Electric had a superb team and were destined to win the cup three years out of four, but Higher Walton managed to break this domination. The English Electric team were so confident of winning that they had booked a victory celebration at the 'Bull & Royal' public house in Preston. An account of the game in the 'Evening Post' said that English Electric were the better footballing side but Higher Walton won with a combination of hard tackling and good luck. Higher Walton had some excellent players. Captain Andy Davies was a brilliant forward who had played in the Lancashire Combination for Netherfield and

The Guildhall Cup
(photograph courtesy
of Roy Rich)

Skelmersdale, and Jack Knowles had played in the Lancashire Combination for Chorley. Bill Gallagher was a centre half who had been closely watched by PNE but had refused to sign as a full-time professional. Goalkeeper Keith Farnworth had played as a professional for Chorley the previous season and, according to Frank Counsell, English Electric tried to make an issue of this with the league, but all the relevant paperwork was correct.

The following match report appeared in the 'Lancashire Evening Post' on Tuesday 3rd May 1960.

GUILDHALL CUP GOES TO HIGHER WALTON

By beating English Electric 2-0 at Deepdale last night Higher Walton United have won the Guildhall Cup for the first time in their history. In doing so they robbed English Electric, Preston & District League Champions, of the prized cup and league double, which they were seeking. In the opening stages of the game the slick moving English Electric side just had the edge over their hard tackling opponents. In the eighth minute, however, Higher Walton surprisingly went into the lead when their skipper Davies crashed home a centre from right-winger Knowles. Electric fought back strongly in their bid for an equaliser and right-winger Gillibrand nearly scored when he sent in a tremendous shot that shaved the top of the crossbar. Halfway through the first half there was a remarkable incident in the Higher Walton goalmouth. The referee gave a goal to English Electric after the ball had been scrambled off the line but after protests from the Higher Walton players he consulted a linesman and to everyone's astonishment he reversed the decision and gave a goal kick to Higher Walton. Undeterred by this setback English Electric again attacked strongly and within two minutes they had scored again but the goal was again disallowed, this time for offside.

STRONG DEFENCE

Play in the second half deteriorated and petty fouls became more frequent, particularly from Higher Walton. English Electric exerted great pressure on the Higher Walton Defence but Coupe and Gallagher excelled in a defence, which never showed the slightest sign of yielding to the swift-moving attack of their opponents.

Slater and Almond were the brains behind the constant English Electric attacks, and Wharton gave a flawless display at centre half. O'Mahoney came close for scoring for English Electric but after dribbling past keeper Farnworth he ran the ball out of play. The English Electric goal had a narrow escape midway through the second half when full back Smethurst nearly put through his own goal. With only two minutes to play outside left Walmsley scored again for Higher Walton and the issue was settled beyond doubt. The trophy was presented by Mr JH Ingham vice-chairman of Preston North End FC

Higher Walton Utd- Keith Farnworth, John Mahoney, David Hayes, Joe Coupe, Bill Gallagher, Frank Harrison, Jack Knowles. Andy Davies, Jack Francis, Norbert Walmsley, Michael Airey.

English Electric- Pallett, Smethurst, Reid, Buckley, Wharton, Slater, Gillibrand, Greenbank, O'Mahoney, Almond, Churchman.

Referee:Mr G.Singleton.

HIGHER WALTON UNITED 1959-60, GUILDHALL CUP WINNERS
Back row, left to right: Tom Counsell (secretary), John Mahoney, Joe Coupe, Keith Farnworth, Frank Harrison, David Hayes, William Harrison (trainer). Front row, left to right: Jack Knowles, Jack Francis, Andy Davies, Norbert Walmsley, Michael Airey. Mascot: Alan Law.   (photograph supplied by the late Bob Burns)

Forty five years later, in 2005, Norbert Walmsley and Joe Coupe were still playing for Higher Walton, but now as crown green bowlers for Higher Walton Bowling Club.

Pastures new.

Not long after this Cup success, at the end of the 1960-61 season, Higher Walton United decided to leave the Preston & District League and join the Blackburn & District Combination. The reason, according to Frank Counsell, was that the team had gone as far as it could and was looking for new challenges. They were to remain there for ten seasons but would never reach the heights achieved in the Preston & District League.

Changing rooms.

During the 1960s, the Higher Walton committee tried to improve the changing facilities for the team. Just before the Second World War, in 1938, plans had been put forward by Walton-le-Dale Urban District Council to build proper changing facilities and tennis courts on King George V playing fields. However, these plans were shelved during wartime and were not revived after the war. The old wooden changing pavilion on King George V playing fields had seen better days so, in 1966, a new changing cabin was purchased by the football club for about £150. This was erected on the land to the right of the present community hall, which was built in later years. The council had initially refused planning permission but, on investigation, it came to light that the councillors on the planning committee knew nothing about this decision. Permission was eventually granted but Higher Walton missed out on a cash grant from the Playing Field Association. The committee members worked hard to paint and put electricity into the new changing rooms. Forty years on, the Council have still not built a proper brick changing facility at King George V playing fields. South Ribble Borough Council now supplies a converted metal container as changing rooms. Things were probably better 50 years ago!

The Mens' Institute building in the 1960s. John Taberner had bought the premises from the Dewhurst Company in the late 1930s and it became a hardware shop until 1986.

(Photograph reproduced with permission of Gill Dimmock)

The committee in 1966 included Tom Counsell, Frank Counsell, Jimmy Crook, Joe Clifton, Eddie Swales, Terry Robertson, Jimmy Tuson and Ray Hardacre. They held regular meetings at the *'Swan Inn'* in Higher Walton to select the team and discuss other matters.

Here are some items mentioned in the minute book of 1966-67, not long after England's World Cup triumph:

Oct. 11th The new cabin has been erected. It was decided to paint it and put in electricity on Saturday. Oct.18th It was proposed to pay travel expenses to players living outside the area. Nov. 1st It was decided to have a chairman for meetings. Tom Counsell agreed to take this position. Nov.29th. A loan of £50 was made to a player, who agreed to repay this at £2 per week. [This was later to prove to be a problem as the player soon fell behind in his payments] Feb. 7th The club was looking into insurance for the cabin. The club asked Hubert Woods if he would mark the pitch for every home game and [the] club would pay him 10/-. He agreed. April 11th Goalkeeper David Halliwell was taken on by PNE without them first approaching the club. The Committee wrote a letter of complaint to PNE. April 19th. It was decided to give the players a night out at the end of the season. It will be held at the 'Swan Inn', with sandwiches & pies. PNE had sent a letter of apology concerning the player Halliwell. May 9th. Club would apply to Council for some grass seed to reseed the pitch. The Club [was] to look into making an aluminium box for carrying the kit instead of the old suitcase.

HIGHER WALTON UNITED 1971-2, EDDLESTON CUP WINNERS.
Back row, l to r: Frank Counsell, Bert Fisher, Eddie Ryding, S.Clemson,Tony Large, Ray Houghton, Brian Costigan, Gerard Higham, Tom Counsell, Harold Wilson (manager). Front row: not known, Tony Beswick, Ken Coupe (capt), Neil Wilson (mascot), Keith Ashcroft, Alan Fawcett, Billy Hardacre.

(photograph supplied by Harold Wilson)

Higher Walton United played mainly in the second division of the *'Blackburn & District Football Combination'*, with fixtures against teams from Darwen, Haslingden, Rishton, Waddington, Pleckgate, Feniscowles, Langho, Ribchester, and Oswaldtwistle. They rarely challenged for league honours but they did win the *'Eddleston Cup'* in the 1971-72 season. Each division of the Blackburn Combination has a different cup and this one is for second division teams.

Return to Preston.

The move to the Blackburn league had not proved to be a success. Several good players had left the club because they preferred to play against teams from the Preston area so, in the 1972–73 season, Higher Walton returned to the Preston & District League.

Higher Walton United were champions of division 1 in their first season back in the Preston & District League but promotion to the Premier division proved to be a disaster. Several good players left the team and, for the next few seasons, the team struggled.

In the 1973-4 season the team's record was played 28, won 2, lost 26, with only 26 goals scored and 119 conceded. The following season was little better: played 30, won 3, drawn 4 and lost 23. Finally in the 1975-76 season all the first 8 games were lost and the team withdrew completely from the senior league. The committee persuaded the League to let them enter a team in the youth division for the rest of the season. Fifteen games out of sixteen in the youth division were also lost, the team conceding 134 goals and scoring only 16! A second dismal season in the youth division followed (played 18, won 2, drawn 2, lost 14, goals for 28, goals against 106, points 6) but the team re-entered the senior division 5 of the Preston & District league in 1977-78. Results steadily improved and the *'Dodgson Shield'* was won in 1980. Higher Walton football was on the rise again!

What the Butler scored.

In 1984 a forward called Kevin Butler signed for the Club. He had just come out of the Army and was intending to play for Bamber Bridge FC, who also played on King George's field at that time. He chose Higher Walton instead. In his first season he scored 27 goals and was leading scorer for 6 seasons, peaking at 37 goals in the 1988-89 season. In the 1984-5 season Higher Walton reached the final of the *'Lancastrian Brigade Cup'*, a supplementary cup competition for teams knocked out of the *'Guildhall Cup'*, but they lost 2-1 to Penwortham St.Teresa's.

Stalwarts retire.

After the relative success of the 1980s, the 1990s marked another decline in Higher Walton's fortunes and by the 1994-5 season they

could only manage one win in 30 games, albeit in division 1. In the mid-90s, secretary Frank Counsell and manager Harold Wilson both decided to retire. Harold had been with the club since the 1970s. He had been a Lancashire Combination referee and a Football League linesman before becoming the Higher Walton team manager. Harold and Frank were typical of the volunteers who keep grassroots football alive.

The late Frank Counsell photographed in 2004

Frank Counsell left the club in 1996. He had joined as a player in 1956, took over as secretary from his father in 1966 and remained as secretary for the next 30 years. He deservedly won the Preston and District League's *'Secretary of the Year'* award in 1993-4. Frank's contribution to local football was immense and he never fully received the recognition which he truly deserved.

The final chapter.

In 1997 the running of the team was taken over by ex-player Malcolm Crowther, who had been with the club without a break since the 1982-83 season.

At first Malcolm was a *'one-man committee,'* being secretary, treasurer and manager all rolled into one, but running a football team on your own is hard work and there were times when Malcolm considered calling it a day. However, in 1999 some players offered to share the load, with Gary Caton taking over as manager, and Steve McKenzie and Peter Dagger assisting. Malcolm continued as secretary/treasurer and the team went from strength to strength. New players were brought in and the team started playing with increased confidence.

Malcolm Crowther

In the 2001-2 season they were promoted as champions of division 2 (East), and the following season were champions of the first division. In that season they also reached the final of the *'Guildhall Cup'*, losing to 5-1 to Burscough Richmond. The following season (2003-4) they played in the Premier division and again reached the final of the *'Guildhall Cup'*. However, they were unable to overcome their rivals, Burscough, and lost 3-1.

HIGHER WALTON UNITED 2003-4, GUILDHALL CUP FINALISTS.
Back row, left to right: Gary Caton (manager), Vinny Vaccaro, Andy Richards, Donny Bolton, Tony Jones, Ronnie Mellor, Billy Slinger, Steve McKenzie, Malcolm Crowther (secretary).
Front: David Harrison, Neil Meadowcroft, Rob Hand, Darren Parkinson, Peter Dagger (captain), Gary Cawood, Damien Whiteside.   (photograph supplied by Roy Rich)

The final whistle.

The village team had reached another of the high points in its long history, but the following season, 2004-05, was to be the last one for Higher Walton United. The manager, Gary Caton, decided to retire and although secretary Malcolm Crowther tried hard, he was unable to find a replacement. He reluctantly withdrew the club from the Preston & District League and the team disbanded. However, we can be sure that it will not be long before Higher Walton Football Club is reborn to continue the long tradition of football in this Lancashire village, and again we can say *"Play up, Higher Walton!"*

BIBLIOGRAPHY:

Newspaper reports from the *'Lancashire Daily Post'*, the *'Preston Herald'* and the *'Preston Guardian'*. (Harris Reference Library, Preston).

Other newspaper reports (the Colindale Library, London)

'A History of Walton-Le -Dale and Bamber Bridge' by David Hunt, 1997.

'A nostalgic and historical walk around Moon's Mill' by Anne Bradley, 1991.

'Our Country Churches and Chapels' by Anthony Hewitson, 1872.

'The Football Annual' 1882 to1895. (National Football Museum collection)

'Blackburn Rovers, the Official Encyclopaedia' by Mike Jackman, 1994.

'Lancashire Daily Post' handbooks, 1920s and 1930s.

(National Football Museum and Dick Clegg collections)

Preston & District League handbooks, 1950 to 2002 (Fred Southern)

All Saints, Higher Walton, school logbooks (Lancashire Record Office)

Census returns for 1881, 1891 and 1901 (Lancashire Record Office)

'All the Lads. A complete who's who of Sunderland FC' by Garth Dykes & Douglas Lamming, 1999.

'History of the Lancashire FA, 1878-1928', C.Sutcliffe & F.Hargreaves, 1928.

'History of Blackburn Rovers 1875-1925' by Charles Francis, 1925.

Preston North End gatebooks for the 1930s (National Football Museum)

'Preston & District Football League 75th Anniversary' by Fred Southern, 1979.

Lancashire FA minute books (Lancashire FA, Leyland)